ADVENTURES OF A WANDERER

Covering the period between the Boer War and the end of the First World War, *Adventures of a Wanderer* is the enthralling and captivating memoir of an extraordinary man with the desire to travel: from South Africa to Australia, from New Zealand to the South Sea Islands, from adventures in Cairo to drinking with the future Mahatma Gandhi in a Durban bar.

Powell's zest and indefatigable spirit of adventure show through his many carefully chosen anecdotes and amusing recollections, but there are also more serious reflections about relations between races and creeds in the countries he visits, springing from both his knowledge and affection.

Set in the great tradition of British travel writing, *Adventures of a Wanderer* provides a unique and fascinating portrait of the life of a traveller before the Great War.

Adventures of a Wanderer is reprinted in paperback for the first time and includes his poem *Gallipoli*. There is a new introduction by Colonel Geoffrey Powell, distinguished soldier and military historian, and author of a number of books including the highly-acclaimed *The Devil's Birthday: The Bridges to Arnhem 1944*.

GW00750447

TO
N. S. P.
AND
OLD FRIENDS
ALL THE WORLD OVER

The cover illustration is taken from '*A Settler's Hut,
near Eagle Hawk Neck, Tasmania*' by J. Haughton For-
rest

ADVENTURES
OF A
WANDERER

BY
SYDNEY WALTER POWELL

Introduced by Colonel Geoffrey Powell and
including the epic poem, *Gallipoli*

Century Hutchinson Ltd
London Melbourne Auckland Johannesburg

First published in 1928 by Jonathan Cape Ltd

This edition first published in 1986 by Century Hutchinson Ltd,
Brookmount House, 62–65 Chandos Place, London, WC2N 4NW

Century Hutchinson Publishing Group (Australia) Pty Ltd
PO Box 496, 16–22 Church Street, Hawthorn, Melbourne, Victoria 3122

Century Hutchinson Group (NZ) Ltd
PO Box 40-086, 32–34 View Road, Glenfield, Auckland 10

Century Hutchinson Group (SA) Pty Ltd
PO Box 337, Berglvei 2012, South Africa

ISBN 0 7126 9469 2

Gallipoli first published in 1933 by the *Poetry Review*

Printed in Great Britain by
Richard Clay ('The Chaucer Press) Ltd, Bungay, Suffolk

INTRODUCTION

BORN seven years after the end of the Franco-Prussian War, Sydney Walter Powell died the year Queen Elizabeth the Second was crowned. He divided his youth, as he put it, into 'the sacred and the profane': the *Adventures of a Wanderer* covers his eighteen years of profanity from the Boer War to the end of the First World War. A further and unpublished autobiography, written about 1942, a decade and a half after this book was published, recounts the story of his earlier and later life. His *South Sea Diary* elaborates on his years in Tahiti, and his novel, *Ancestors*, is a thinly disguised account of his family background. As his nephew, who enjoyed his company from time to time towards the end of his life, I can fill in a few gaps.

The atmosphere in which Powell was raised was, in fact, far less sacred than that of many similar Victorian professional families. The second son of a London architect with a rapidly rising reputation, he was brought up in a tall Georgian house in Mecklenburg Square, his childhood 'remarkably placid, as placid as the old square with its plane trees and almost total freedom from traffic'. In contrast, the back of the house touched the Gray's Inn Road, down which the clanging of iron tyres and iron-shod hoofs on the stone paving-blocks produced a din far greater than the present-day roar of internal-combustion engines. But walking was the main means of progression. From Bloomsbury his nurse took him daily on foot to the West End parks, and when he was a little older his father delighted in exploring with him the streets of London – from the slums of Blackfriars to St. John's Wood, where a skull-capped great-uncle regaled the two of them on plum-cake and port.

In most ways the author's father was a kindly and considerate man, but he flouted the conventions of the day in a way that was to prove disasterous. As his son was to write, 'The history of our family was a history of the undesigned, of bolts, often calamitous, out of the blue.' And bolt his father did, to the Channel Islands with a barrister's wife, unacceptable conduct in the 1880s for a professional man. The barrister sued for divorce, and the case was reported in the so-called reputable press in the usual salacious manner of the time. The architectural practice collapsed, and William Powell moved to South Africa with his eldest son to start a fresh career. Fortunately for the family, the affair proved short-lived, and after three years the author's mother decided to join her husband in Natal, bringing with her their three younger sons. There she found him well-established once again, designing what were to be some of the major public buildings of Durban and Pietermaritzburg. The following year a fifth son was born.

Aldenham, where Sydney Powell spent three years before sailing for South Africa, was not as starkly Spartan as many Victorian public schools, despite the unheated chapel and classrooms. Food was plentiful, beer was served twice a day, and there was unlimited (and intoxicating) claret-cup at the end-of-term suppers. Compulsory games were minimal, fortunately for Powell, who lacked both interest and talent, but on several afternoons each week boys could roam the countryside at will. He was a quiet boy whose academic accomplishments matched his athletic abilities. Already, however, he had shown indications of an adventurous streak (he had run away from his prep school more from devilment than through unhappiness) and, with some justification, he was in later years to reflect that 'the noisiest boys were often at heart the tamest, the quiet ones the most adventurous'.

After the cold of an Aldenham winter, Powell was conscious of a glorious change in his life when he arrived in South Africa. He took unalloyed pleasure in the tropical richness of Durban, an atmosphere which stimulated all his senses and where he never experienced disillusionment. He throve mentally and physically in the relaxed life-style, and he shared with his father an artist's delight in the beauty that surrounded them. But close as father and son were, their characters were too similar, and they often quarrelled. When his father refused to allow Sydney to serve his articles as an architect with him, his son refused to study under

INTRODUCTION

someone he knew to be a lesser man, declaring that he would either work under the best man in South Africa or look for a career elsewhere. And so he entered the Natal Civil Service, which offered in his words, 'a career of sorts and it was gentlemanly'. With hours from nine to four, and not much work to fill them, he had time to write, a craft in which he had been encouraged by the publication (fee: one guinea) of a sonnet in the long extinct *Temple Bar* magazine. The *Adventures of a Wanderer* begins with his severance from this safe career with its prospects of an under-secretaryship and a C.M.G. and its certain pension.

So started the 'profane' period, more the consequence of boredom and whim than deliberate intention. It was 'rather my compromise with circumstances'. Boredom was always to be his spur: he did not seek adventure, but adventure came his way. For all that, the zest which shines through the pages of this book and that sparkles in his eyes when, in his old age, he reminisced are proof that he revelled in his wandering years despite all the hardship and sickness he encountered. 'Life had been very kind to me in these last eighteen years,' he was to write. And to use his own words again, 'The most devastating sensual indulgence is that of ambition. By it a man loses not only his own soul but the world, and finds himself left with a spectre.' 'The happiest state,' he had decided, 'was not wanting anything.'

It was a simple matter to travel before the First World War. You bought a ticket and boarded a ship. When you arrived, you sought work. Passports were all but unknown. Denys Reitz, the South African soldier and statesman, who in 1902 went into exile after the Boer surrender rather than live under the British (he was to end the next war commanding a battalion of the King's Shropshire Light Infantry on the Western Front), had never even heard the word 'passport' when he tried to enter Portugese East Africa in 1902. Forty years or so later, Ernest Bevin, then Foreign Secretary to Attlee, enshrined his foreign policy in the words 'to be able to go to Victoria Station and buy a railway ticket to anywhere he bloody-well chose'. The impractibility of such an

INTRODUCTION

ambition today is perhaps the measure of the world in which we live.

One is struck by the background of many of the author's friends and associates during his travels. Like possibly attracted like, but Kipling's 'gentleman rankers' were thick on the ground – the Swedish count in the Cape Mounted Rifles, the Household Cavalry doctor on the Cape Town docks, the Harrow man in the Australian bush, the high proportion of public school men in the British South African Police in Rhodesia, as there had been in the Cape Mounted Rifles. Half his Australian tent-mates in the camp by the Pyramids were of similar stamp. Britain lacked jobs of what was thought to be proper status for the sons of large Victorian middle-class families, and a number left to seek their fortune in the expanding Empire. Once there many sank without trace; class fluidity was high.

Sydney Powell mixed easily with all classes, and with all races. However, many readers of this book, published half a century ago, may be shocked by his matter-of-fact use of the word 'kaffirs' to describe South Africa's black population. Merely the Arabic word for 'unbeliever', it was at the time an acceptable term and lacked pejorative connotations. In fact, 'British Kaffraria' was at the turn of the century the official title of the black reserves. Powell also sounds condescending when discussing Jews that he met, but in this he was no more than a man of his time. His own words, 'In considering history one should always get out of our skins and into the skins of our predecessors,' are apt. He has written elsewhere of his pleasure at an absence of a colour-bar in Tahiti. Not that he observed such restrictions even in their citadel: when he again encountered the future Mahatma Gandhi after the stretcher bearer unit in which they had served together had been disbanded, they adjourned to a Durban bar for a drink. He respected all men for what they were, regardless of the colour of their skins, and he loved the people of Tahiti with whom he lived on equal terms. Rude he may be about the Egyptians in the Cairo brothel quarter, but he is even ruder about

INTRODUCTION

the manners and characteristics of the white tourists who even then were starting to despoil Tahiti; and while he is critical about such people in this book, elsewhere he is virulent.

The author describes a British acquaintance in Papeete as 'the ideal cut of a cavalryman – broad shouldered, narrow flanked and long in the leg'. This is a self-portrait. There is small doubt that women found him hard to resist, and he had considerable difficulty in resisting them. Much of his early life was indeed enjoyably profane. He admitted that he 'wined and wenched like other young men', and whenever he had collected a few pounds together they quickly slipped through his hands. He could look after himself in a bar-room brawl, and whenever army life bored him he quickly went 'absent without leave'. It was, as he said, a habit. He could skip easily into the life of a barrack-room or a New Zealand rabbit-poisoning gang, but he was equally, or more, happy in his own company. Digging alone for months at a time in the Kauri-gum fields, he 'enjoyed the retirement with its opportunities for uninterrupted thought'. But after a time, when he 'had skimmed the cream from his solitude', he would make for civilisation again to burn his money.

This book ends as the author sails from Tahiti for the second time, never to return. The 'engagement' which it was his purpose to fulfil was a play on words. He left to marry the quiet and gentle Highland nurse who had cared for him as he recovered from his Gallipoli wounds. The couple came together again in Australia as the war was ending. By the time she arrived he had settled down to scratch a living writing novels for the railway book-stall trade. With a small legacy they bought an isolated cottage in the Blue Mountains, where their nearest neighbours were Norman Lindsay the artist and writer, and his wife. The two men, both in their way recluses, became intimate friends, although they could quarrel fiercely, usually on literary questions. Like Lindsay, Powell easily took offence.

Throughout his adult life, whenever opportunity offered, Powell had written. As a slothful civil servant in Natal, and later

INTRODUCTION

as a soldier during the Boer War, he had contributed to a Durban paper and he also wrote the first guide-book to Durban. Again as a soldier, on Thursday island, he had written verse and short stories which were published in the *Sydney Bulletin*. As a night-watchman during his second visit to Tahiti, he found his time for writing had been unlimited. Then, in the Blue Mountains, he showed Lindsay the manuscript of a serious novel he had completed. Sent to a London publisher recommended by Lindsay, it was accepted with enthusiasm. A literary career beckoned, and England seemed the only place to develop it. In 1925, he and his wife sold up and left, a decision Powell was to query to the end of his days.

As they moved from cottage to cottage, sometimes around Salisbury, sometimes in Bournemouth, life continued to be migratory. Over a period of twenty years he wrote and published eighteen books, and he and his wife existed upon the spasmodic and small advances and royalty cheques. Review work for the *Times Literary Supplement* helped stave off penury. Most of his novels had as their background either the South Seas or contemporary England, but his interests ranged wide – from philosophy to Egyptology, from the Greeks to graphology. That Conrad was his mentor is clear from his prose, and in this he took pride; but his poetry belonged to no particular school.

Recognition as a poet came about in the following manner. Despairing of his work ever being published, in 1932 he entered his epic poem *Gallipoli* for a festival for poets under forty years of age which John Masefield, the poet Laureate, was organising. Awarded the first prize in the competition, Powell, well over the age limit, then 54, admitted to the deception by return of post and gave back the prize cheque of £25. Masefield was understandably annoyed, but the ruse succeeded. The following year the *Poetry Review* published the poem, and in 1934 Harrap brought out a collection of Powell's poetical work, *One Way Street*. Fifty years ago it was no more easy for an unknown poet to be published by a major house than it is today. For three or

INTRODUCTION

four years Powell wrote leading articles and reviews for *Poetry Review*, but something went amiss, and he severed his connections one day in a rage.

And so Powell's life drifted gently towards its end. Happy enough in the society of his wife, he could blossom when any member of his family broke into his seclusion. Otherwise his pen was his outlet. He was always nostalgic for the South Seas, their warmth and their colour. For all his dislike of criticism, he described himself correctly as a modest man, and this once hero-worshipping and now elderly nephew would give much to sit opposite him again, fire glowing and whisky glass in hand, listening to the self-effacing stories of his wandering years and his philosophy on how life should be lived.

He died in 1952, a few months after losing his wife.

Geoffrey Powell
1986

NOTE

THIS book is not fiction. In it I have written the story of my roving years. As much of its detail would not interest the reader, I have selected, expanding here, condensing there, but never inventing nor falsifying, except where names have been changed for obvious reasons.

Years have passed since I was first urged to write this book. I am glad that I did not write it then, for I should certainly have wasted good material. Whether I should still have waited I leave others to judge.

S. W. P.

ADVENTURES OF A WANDERER

CHAPTER I

★

§ 1

ABOUT the middle of the year 1901 I stood upon the rim of a cup of hills, looking down on the township of Umtata in British Kaffraria. It was for the moment my goal, and my feelings were much those of a freebooter surveying his objective. Umtata had to supply me with food and drink, with a lodging and with money to continue my journey. I was on foot, I had three shillings in my pocket, and I had travelled a hundred miles in less than a week, under a hot sun and carrying my belongings on my back in a cloth hold-all. My shoulders were sore, my feet were sorer; I was thirsty and the sweat had dried upon me, so that all my skin was salt; but the townsmen's roofs were in sight and I was glad.

Before I descend I had better give an account of how I came here. The outbreak of the South African War had found me a discontented clerk in the Civil Service of Natal. I was then twenty-one. For long I had been beset by a mortal disgust, a passionate impatience with my life; a feeling that it was not life but death to me. Some wild strain in me revolted against quietly pacing the smooth road which led to a chief clerkship; possibly to a C.M.G. and an under-secretaryship; certainly to a pension. To get there I was to endure a drab existence; and it appeared to me that unless one lived colorously it was not worth while to be alive.

At the opening of the war I applied for leave; it was

refused, and I resigned; and forthwith I embarked on a
life of adventure, to last for eighteen years. I may say
here that this life of adventure was not my ideal of life;
it was rather my compromise with circumstances. The
dreams, the longings of boyhood had been swept away;
the ungarnished world had an ugly look; and I had to
make the best of it, to make it habitable.

An Indian ambulance corps which wanted leaders was
my means of going to the front, and in it I made the
acquaintance of a young barrister whom I chiefly remember on account of his devotion to duty and his loving care
for his men. His name was Gandhi. With Buller's army
we marched and countermarched: but the campaign of
the Ladysmith relief force is now a threadbare story, and
my own part in it not of sufficient interest to justify nar-
ration. For a great part of the time I was a spectator,
hugely enjoying the show and my freedom from office
walls; and I found leisure to write for a Natal newspaper
with which I had a connection.

After the relief my corps was disbanded, and I had a
year of civilian life, during which I lived part of the time
by journalism and the remainder as a clerk in a special
government department created by the war. It had a staff
of two and was very snug; but unrest again seized me. I
conceived the idea of walking to East London, and accordingly set out from Durban with a few shillings in my
pocket. My intention on arrival was to enlist in one of the
various mounted irregular corps, but this opportunity presented itself at Kokstad, the capital of East Griqualand.

to which I came after a ten days' tramp. I was fated throughout this war to join units which within six months were disbanded. In East Griqualand I served for five months, without seeing an enemy.

On receiving my discharge I spent a week and most of my pay in Kokstad, and left there with a sovereign and, I believe, a headache. It was quite a small town, but by no means slow, and willing to be accelerated. Thence, without notable adventure, I came to that ring of hills encircling Umtata. Here I was to pause before starting on my final stage to the coast.

The day was closing as I descended the hill; the shadows rose around me on the bare slopes, and soon the last of the sunlight vanished from the summits. I crossed a bridge in the dusk and came directly upon the tin-roofed, straggling town. A slowly-moving ox-wagon was just ahead of me. The first house I came to was, to my satisfaction, a hotel, as a glimpse of the bar informed me. There was nothing else to distinguish it from any other rambling wooden bungalow.

My plans were already formed, and I needed only nerve and good fortune to carry them out successfully. The nerve I felt I had; the good fortune I could not count upon.

Into the bar, then, I bowled; deposited my hold-all on a settle, and called for a glass of beer. I paid for it, drank it, and ordered another.

'I want a room,' I said to the landlord, who was serving.

'I can put you up,' he answered. 'You came in that wagon, did you?'

'I came on foot,' I replied, and slapped my second shilling on the counter. That left me with one. 'When will dinner be on?' I asked.

'In about ten minutes,' said the landlord. 'I'll show you your room now, if you want a brush-up.'

I went with him, and shortly afterwards entered the dining-room, washed and newly arrayed.

This, the first part of my scheme of operations, was easily accomplished. The crisis would come to-morrow. I had to obtain a job, you see; not only to pay my hotel bill, but to take me to East London. I might have pushed on without money, but I was loth to do so; and anyhow I wished to break my journey again. A month's employment in Umtata would both rest me and give me ample funds for the road, and clerical employment was not usually hard to get in South Africa, outside the large cities and the beaten tracks. Still, one could not always get it at a moment's notice.

I made an excellent dinner, drank another glass of beer (signing a card for it, as I wished to keep my last shilling), and retired to bed at an early hour, with gusto, for I had not slept between sheets for many days. In the morning I shaved and dressed with care: my linen was clean, my suit old but decent and well cut. My boots were new, and impressively respectable when polished. I was going to fly high at my first attempt. I was calling upon no less a person than the Commissioner for the Territory.

I need not detail our interview. I produced my Natal Civil Service papers, and as far as they went they were quite satisfactory; he asked me, among other questions, how I had come here, and I again recklessly stated that I had walked. Honesty, however, upon this point, was really the best policy, Umtata being so small a place that all arrivals were noted; and South Africa was indulgent to eccentrics in those days. They were so many, and so many of them were good men. Finally the chief, having looked me over, asked me for my address, and told me I should hear from him in an hour or two. I retired, very hopeful, and before noon a uniformed kaffir brought me a letter. I opened the blue envelope. It contained a **temporary clerical appointment**. I was to start on the morrow.

I lightly informed my landlord of the occurrence, and said I should be staying with him.

§ 2

I divide my youth into two periods, the sacred and the profane. Of the first I have never written and am not likely to write. I was now in the full bloom of my profane period – three and twenty, a glorious age.

My temporary clerical position proved all that could be desired; there were good fellows in the office, and I settled to work. I determined, however, to stay no more than a month. I was not taking up office work again as a permanent means of livelihood. On that point I was firmly resolved, and so at the end of three weeks I gave notice of my intention. I fear that the Commissioner was greatly and reasonably disappointed in me; but, at any rate, I went.

I had twelve pounds; seven I owed to the hotel (it had, by the way, changed hands shortly after my arrival), which left me well provided for my journey. A smart young Jew was now the hotel's proprietor: I told him I was leaving the next morning and would pay my account then. He was from Johannesburg, and wore invariably check riding-breeches and Stohwasser gaiters; but his horsey air was delusive; he was a boxing-man, and had fought in the Johannesburg ring. Whether he bought the hotel from the proceeds of his victories I never learned; but from subsequent experience I should say not.

That evening I fell in with some Cape Mounted Riflemen, merry blades with whom I was already acquainted. The ensuing proceedings took the form of a farewell jollification, and so convivial were we that I woke next morning with my capital reduced to twenty-two shillings. How I spent eleven pounds I have no idea, but I doubt not that we had value for them. The C.M.R. fellows, I think, were short of money, but they had been very hospitable to me in the past. The calamity was a just judgment upon me, for I had promised to meet that night a girl, who had brightened my stay in Umtata.

I was sorry that I could not pay my bill, and sorry for my own loss, but regrets were idle, and I suppressed them. I had to think quickly. Pride forbade that I should go to the Commissioner and ask to be re-engaged. To that the only alternative was to bolt; and as there was nothing to be gained by loitering, I packed my bag and made an instant departure. Mine being an outside room I was able to escape unnoticed.

It was now about 10 a.m. and I avoided the main thoroughfare. I did not know if Samuel, my late host, was in the hotel or out. Usually he was in the bar at this time. On this particular morning, as it happened, he was not.

I got safely through the town and was near the top of a rise upon the outskirts when I heard a shout behind me. I looked round and at the foot of the rise saw Samuel with another man, whom I recognized as a Swedish count in the C.M.R. Despite his nobility, he was an officer's servant and was in mufti. My creditor was shouting to me, and when I looked round he waved his hand. I responded, but quickened my pace a little. At that he began to run, the count accompanying him, and I followed their example. Laden though I was I made good going, and a bend of the road hiding me for a moment, I dashed up a path and in at the open door of a cottage. I met nobody until I was in the back yard, where there was a girl, to whom I apologized for taking a short cut. It was a short cut, which was why I had taken it, for the road wound from the front to the rear of the cottage. To tell the truth, I was strongly disinclined to face the fighting Jew and his Swedish ally. Scaling the back-yard fence with remarkable agility, I was soon upon the road on the other side. I had gained a quarter of a mile by my manœuvre.

I proceeded at a more moderate pace, and looking behind me frequently, at last discerned the pair a good half-mile away. Again they halted, and this time I had the satisfaction of seeing them turn back. Believing that they had finally abandoned the chase, I rested awhile by the roadside and then pushed on.

Hot and thirsty beyond words, I arrived in the afternoon at an inn. I had had neither breakfast nor lunch, so was faint besides, and I ate bread and cheese and drank Bavarian beer. I was no more than eight miles from my starting-point, but I had walked slowly and rested often, as I was feeling the effects of last night's merry-making. In these circumstances the Bavarian was very soothing, and I drank several bottles of it, though aware that I must husband my money as well as I could. But the expense appeared to be justified, for sitting in that cool and pleasant bar I felt myself reviving. I was the only customer, and the landlord served me. I recall him clearly, a big, brown-bearded man, rather lethargic.

I sat by a window commanding a view of the road and the sun-burned veldt; and in a state of mind now almost blissful, I heard carriage-wheels. I heard them with a lazy and unsuspicious ear. The carriage came in sight. It was a two-horsed spider and had three occupants. They were Samuel, his wife and the count. The spider pulled up under a tree, and the gentlemen got out, leaving the lady.

Well, I can usually rise to an occasion, and I waited with desperate calm for the approaching scene. The two men were coming, of course, to the inn, and I made no doubt that they had tracked me or guessed my where-abouts. Why the count, with whom I had been on good terms, should join in the pursuit of me, I could not imagine; unless it was that he was on better terms with Samuel, which probably was the case.

They came straight into the bar, Samuel leading, and the latter paused in the doorway.

'Here he is,' he said over his shoulder, and there was in his voice a ring of anticipatory satisfaction which warned me to prepare for the worst.

I sat still. It was not for me to take the offensive; and I saw no reason why I should precipitate my own slaughter.

Without asking for an explanation he walked up to me, and before I could move he hit me.

It was a light blow with just enough sting in it to bring me to my feet at a leap by a process of reflex action. The blow I returned him was not a light one; a second brought him down. The count's face told of his amazement, but my own was greater; it had no limits. I should mention that the count, evidently alarmed for my safety, perhaps for my life, had attempted to restrain Samuel when he stepped up to me.

The pugilist rose, himself surprised, but game. He was just about my weight, but an inch or two shorter, and I had the advantage of reach. The room was very small, and with settles and a table in a corner and the bar projecting into it, so little space was left that ring tactics were impossible. I again adopted the offensive, relying on

25

straight lefts and my superior reach. He went to the floor a second time, but was on his legs once more a moment later. He might as well have stayed where he was, for, flushed with my success and feeling like Tom Sayers, I at once sent him down for the third time, and that ended the fight.

It had occupied, I suppose, about three minutes, and I doubt if he hit me once during its progress. I think we were all three flabbergasted at the result. Assisted to his feet, Samuel held out his hand and said he had had enough. He was bleeding, and the innkeeper, effectually roused from his lethargy and now considerably agitated, supplied a basin of water and a dish-cloth. He must have been as much amazed as anybody, to see two men suddenly at fisticuffs for no apparent reason. The affair was not explained to him; he was ignored. However, he was able to gather what the trouble was about, for I seized the opportunity to acquaint Samuel that I had not intentionally bilked him. The fight had cooled him greatly; he listened sympathetically to me, and called for drinks all round. I recommended the Munich, and a bottle was sent out to Mrs. Samuel, who preferred to sit in the spider. In five minutes we were the happiest little gathering, and Samuel was complimenting me on my straight left and describing what he would have done to me in a ring. He even offered me a return match in the yard, but this I wisely declined. I too had cooled, and I was not so fatuous as to think that I could beat him in the open.

He wished me to return with him to Umtata, promising

to stand by me and help me to find another job. But I disliked the thought of turning back; and he saw that I meant to go on. He then offered to lend me a pound; but I could not take that and increase my debt to him.

So, most amicably, we parted, and the count shook hands very respectfully with me.

They drove off, and we waved adieux.

The sun was setting by this time, and a traveller was drawing near the inn by the road from Umtata. He was on foot and carried what in Australia is termed a swag: that is, a roll of blankets slung to his shoulder. He was some way off, and I did not see him closely until half an hour later, when we met in the yard.

'Jim Hammond!' I exclaimed.

He had been a comrade of mine in the Griqualand corps, and had once been a sergeant in the Gordons. I was very glad to see him, and as we were bound in the same direction (though Hammond was not for East London) we agreed to travel as far as we could together. He had a little money, but was economizing it, and the inn-keeper was allowing him to sleep in a shed. He advised me to ask the same favour, which I did, and was readily obliged. While we were talking in the shed, and before I had given any thought to the question of dinner, our host came in with two full plates of meat and vegetables.

'The missus,' he said to me, 'thought you might like a bit of dinner, and as you aren't too flush we don't expect you to pay for it.'

We expressed our hearty thanks.

27

I had a good horse-blanket in my bag, and slept soundly after the day's fatigues and excitements.

A substantial breakfast put us in good tune for the road, and with pipes alight we started.

CHAPTER II

★

§ 1

HAMMOND was a sturdy old soldier, straight and strong of frame as an oak door, and with features that would have suited a field-marshal. His youth had been dedicated equally to Venus and to Mars, and Nature had well equipped him to serve both deities. Since leaving the Army he had employed himself as a railway-construction ganger, when there was no war to engage him, and had traversed South Africa up and down in pursuit of his occupation. He was now on his way to a job he had heard of in the Cape Colony. He suffered from a common complaint of foot-soldiers, varicose veins, so we had to proceed slowly.

Of the details of that journey I remember little. So many subsequent journeyings, so many greater experiences, have tended to obliterate them. Day after day we followed a winding road that switchbacked over undulating country almost uniform in colour (a dusty brown) but wonderfully diverse in form. It was for the most part treeless, but the nobler for its nudity, and of a splendid spaciousness spread under a cloudless and dazzling sky. There was something primeval in the unadorned majesty of its bareness viewed from the crests of hills, and something poetic in the immense blue distances, which the transparent atmosphere clarified. To the east our vision ranged over the sea of hills for as far as a hundred miles, where its billows melted into the blue of the sky. There were kraals along our route and we drank many draughts of kaffir beer, the most lastingly refreshing of all brews. Throughout South Africa the toothless patriarchs live on kaffir beer, which being made from corn and easily digestible is the perfect food for age. Like beer elsewhere, it varies in strength and quality, but the best, sparkling and cloudy-clear, is nectar.

Sometimes we camped, sometimes we slept in sheds or in rooms at hotels, according to conditions of weather, place and human regard of us. We rarely asked favours, but often received them. We could not afford regular hotel accommodation, but several times we had it without expense.

Two episodes of my journey were not agreeable. I had half a sovereign left when I parted from Hammond, whose road was to the north, and I offered it at a wayside store to pay for some small purchases.

The store-keeper rang it on the counter and said that it was bad.

I was horror-stricken. I saw myself at the best without money to enter East London; at the worst arrested as a passer of counterfeit money. My face must have shown my consternation and saved me from suspicion. I handed back my purchases, and said I was sorry, but that was all the money I had.

The store-keeper then did an extraordinary thing. He put the half-sovereign in his till and gave me my change.

'I'll pass it off on some one else,' he said.

My thanks were incoherent. But my gratitude was deep as I resumed my way.

I came at length to the Kei River, the western boundary of the Transkei, through which I had been travelling. Here there was a hotel and a C.M.R. post, this river being one of the limits of the territory within which the C.M.R. in peace-time operated. I called at the hotel, but the weather being mild I did not seek shelter here, but made my camp by the riverside. I had noticed the proprietor look curiously at me, and, not relishing his attention, had stayed in the bar no longer than to drink a glass of dop. About seven o'clock, when it was dark, a uniformed sergeant and trooper came to my fire.

I was asked where I came from, and replied, 'From Umtata.'

The sergeant then said: 'Your name's So-and-So. You're a deserter from the C.M.R.'

Desertions from the C.M.R. were not infrequent, and many men took French leave during the war, to join the better-paid mounted irregulars. A recognized duty of the troopers at this post was to arrest deserters.

I showed my papers, but the sergeant was not satisfied. I tallied with the description of a deserter, and I had the regular cut, he remarked, of the regiment. (I had been apprised of this when I was at Umtata, where an officer had ordered me to barracks, thinking I was one of his men.) Helpless, I had to go with the sergeant, and I spent that night in a cell.

I remained there till ten o'clock in the morning, when word came through by telegraph that the man for whom I was mistaken had been arrested. The sergeant was profusely apologetic, and I left his post with a quantity of excellent provisions and a bottle of brandy.

I was now in the Cape Colony proper, and finally one night soon after sunset I saw the lights of East London. I should have been jubilant: I was not. I was tired, and I felt very friendless and homeless, in sight of this city; shy too, after eight months in the wilderness. I had five shillings, carefully preserved, to pay for my bed and breakfast and other refreshment. I had walked a long distance that day, and the way through the suburbs seemed endless.

I found a very modest-looking hostelry where I secured a room, and having quenched my thirst retired to bed. No, not to bed but to Heaven.

§ 2

Next morning I breakfasted and then went straight to the Drill Hall, the headquarters of recruiting. Here I came across an officer who proposed that I should join the Q.M.I., and not being particular as to what I joined, I fell in with his wishes. The Q.M.I. was the Queenstown Mounted Infantry, a section, a squadron in strength, of the Cape Defence Force. I passed the doctor, was attested, and sent to the detail camp.

Of all the depressing places on this earth which have come within my experience, I give the palm to detail camps and base camps. The food is always vile, the restrictions harassing, the n.c.o.'s tyrannical, the surroundings cheerless. Fortunately, although I have been in many, I was never long in any of them. This camp I left on the

32

following morning, to entrain for a place called Tarkastad. I had three companions, Cape Colony youths, whom I saw very little of afterwards.

The squadron was encamped in the neighbourhood of Tarkastad, a Dutch village set in the midst of the veldt, and we and our kits were taken out by wagon. We had hardly been inspected by the sergeant-major, when I was summoned to appear before the captain. He was seated in a small tent-wagon, his office, and at once informed me that I was to return to Tarkastad to take over the duties of staff-sergeant and paymaster, from the sergeant who was then fulfilling them, and who in a week was to have his discharge, time-expired. Service in the South African irregulars, I should mention, was for a period of six months only, and a man could then re-engage if he desired. The reason why I had been selected to fill the coming vacancy was that, when being attested, I had stated my occupation as that of a clerk, and the recruiting-officer, aware that a pay-sergeant was needed, had sent a note about me. I was given a horse, and rode back to the village with the quartermaster, my kit going in his wagon. I was not to stay longer in Tarkastad than to learn the routine of my duties and make up the current pay-sheets. I was glad of that, for I had a fancy to see life with the squadron, and was not at first enamoured with the idea of becoming a soldier-clerk.

The present staff-sergeant was quartered at the hotel of a certain Isaacson, and there I too found lodging. Isaacson was a small elderly Hebrew with a gray beard and Petticoat Lane writ large on him; but Isaacson junior was a swell: he had been to Oxford. With no material end in view, it appeared, but solely to acquire culture; for he had left Oxford to return to his father's pub, where he filled the position of barman. His smart tweeds and brilliant socks and neck-ties gave a tone and an exotic touch to the establishment. He served drinks in a bored manner and talked of 'the governor.' Yet he still preserved the virtues of his race. His accent might be the accent of Oxford, but he could gauge the safe length of a credit, and none got under his guard. Old Isaacson was very proud of his son, and I never knew a more touching instance of faith in education for its own sake. He was not, probably, a rich man, and the expense was not even incurred for display, display being impossible in Tarkastad.

I spent six quite agreeable weeks at this place, weeks punctuated by alarums and excursions and one scene of peculiar interest. Several nights we had to man the town defences, and I made a trip to Queenstown, twenty miles off, in charge of an armoured train. The scene of interest was the execution of a rebel. It took place on the sports ground, by unconscious irony. There were few troops in the town, and these were drawn up in extended order on three sides of the square. The commandant and most of the townspeople assembled, and finally the condemned man arrived in a covered cart. He passed within a few paces of me; he was sitting at the back, looking out, and I saw him very clearly. His face — well, his face was that of a man in precisely his situation. He was pale and his

34

expression was that of the doomed. Words will not convey more.

The cart halted in the middle of the ground, where the firing-squad was stationed, and the prisoner stepped down without assistance. There was a chair and by its side a grave, and beyond that a bag of quicklime. He was seated in the chair, and a chaplain spoke with him for a few minutes, after which he was bound to the chair and blindfolded. All being ready, and the chaplain having withdrawn, the officer in command of the firing-party gave the preliminary orders. While at the 'present' a nervous member of the party pulled his trigger; the bullet went wide, and the prisoner, but for his bonds, would have jumped off the chair.

There was a pause. The officer was apparently uncertain what, exactly, to do. At last he gave the order to fire; the rifles crashed, and the body of the victim shuddered and sagged. It was all over; but the poor devil had died twice.

The corpse was then laid in the grave and the quicklime cast on it. The performance was ghastly enough, but the onlookers, mostly Dutch, showed no signs of horror as they dispersed.

At the end of the six weeks my squadron was once more in the neighbourhood. I rejoined it with my pay-sheets all in order; the money was drawn from the bank, and the men were paid.

Thereafter I travelled with the squadron, making up the pay-sheets as occasion served, and acting as orderly-room

35

sergeant. In respect of ordinary duty I was a super-numerary, performing special services such as despatch-carrying. I had a very good pony, a Basuto, the limits of whose endurance I never saw. Sometimes, after riding all day with despatches, I would return to find the squadron starting on a night-march, but though these marches were always rapid movements, intended to surprise the enemy, Tim never failed to carry me to the end. He was a rig, and when off-saddled and turned out, would at once go after the mares. His colour was iron-gray; he had the sure feet of a goat, and cat's eyes in the dark. Ant-bear holes pitted the veldt, and galloping at night was danger-ous, if you had not a horse with eyes for holes and the quickness to avoid them. As for his sure-footedness, I have rattled him down hillsides strewn with loose stones and steep as the roof of a house.

Never have I experienced anything like the weariness that attacked me on those night-rides after a day in the saddle. We would start in the early hours of darkness, in column of route, for a point, it might be, thirty or forty miles away, where the presence of Boers was suspected or had been located. The country in which we were working was very much broken by hills and ravines, so that going was not at all times easy, and horses had often to be led. In the more open country falls were frequent, on account of the ant-bear holes. At intervals we halted and dismounted for no more than a minute or two, and then men would fall asleep beside their horses, and be roused by the pull of the reins as the column moved on.

We even, when at a walk, went to sleep in the saddle, leaning on the horse's neck. It was of course forbidden to smoke, so those of us who could acquire the habit chewed tobacco. I found it to be one of the few vices I could not pleasurably practise. But this prohibition of lights was of little avail, I believe, as the ring of our horses' hoofs, in the stillness, must have been audible miles away. Moonless nights were those chosen; they were usually starry and crisp; and I remember well the dawns. The first faint lightening in the east would come about one or two o'clock. It would grow by extraordinarily slow degrees (tormentingly slow to us), hardly paling the stars until hours later. But it was the promise of the end – of some end, whatsoever – and we espied it gladly. In the gray half-light or earlier we would reach our objective. It might be a tree-shrouded farm or a lonely kopje. If the former, there would be some brief reconnoitring. If the latter, we would surround it, leave our horses with the Number Three's and rush it. On no occasion, when I was with the squadron, did we ever find the enemy on these night-raids. I have an idea that our guides, all 'loyal' Dutchmen, were not entirely trustworthy. They rode always at our commander's side, and he had a revolver ready to shoot them in case of an ambush, which, in the narrow defiles that we had to thread, might easily have resulted in our total destruction.

The ride being at an end, we would off-saddle, feed our horses, put out Cossack posts, and breakfast. Then would follow attempts to sleep in the broiling sun, with not even a blanket for shelter, for we had to ride with stripped saddles. After noon we would start on our way back, unless there was still hope of finding the enemy, when we would lie where we were until the night and make another cast for him.

Sometimes these casts were repeated three nights in succession. Altogether we had more hard work than fighting. Brushes we had, in the daytime, but no serious engagements. My first experience of sharp rifle-fire has left a vivid memory. In Natal I had had no experience of it, though I was often under shell-fire there. I thought, therefore, that I was quite broken to fire (just as I imagined this disturbance in the veldt to be a great war). I had grounds for this belief; for once, by the Tugela, I had lain in my tent a whole afternoon while some Boer guns lobbed shells over and round me, making bad practice at a transport park. I was off duty, the story was interesting, the gun-fire, no new thing, was not; and I felt that I was as likely to be blown up by moving as by staying; but I cannot imagine any novel engrossing me so again.

We were high on the spur of a hill, on that other occasion to which I was alluding. Over against us was a similar spur, and dividing them a small valley, which rose steeply to the junction of the two spurs. The valley was bare, but elsewhere there was plenty of boulders and scrub, giving cover. One of our scouts was riding up the valley. Suddenly we heard a shot from the other side of it, and the man turned his horse and began to race back. We dismounted at once and took cover, and our horses were retired behind the ridge. Below us our scout, crouched forward and riding hell-for-leather, was making an exciting race for life. He was being hotly peppered, and once he reeled in his saddle and we thought he was down. By this time we ourselves were under fire, and it was seen that we should have walked straight into a Boer position but for that first shot. It was the oft-repeated story of an engagement saved or lost by premature shooting. One nervy man had saved us.

As I say, we were under fire, and it was a close fire; it spread like a net about us. We returned it as well as we could, but the enemy had the advantage of having clearly seen us before we dropped down. I was as uncomfortable as I have ever been. I had no inclination to run away, but I was acutely apprehensive of these worse than waspish insects that pinged by me. The fighting in Natal had been, as far as I was concerned, a spectacle, impressive but remote; as for the shells I had soon learned that their bark was worse than their bite. The ping of these bullets was novel and very sinister; and I knew that the danger was no illusion. Another cardinal difference: there was something very intimate and personal about this style of fighting. Individuals were trying to kill individuals. . . . Nevertheless, after ten minutes of it, my sensations became numbed. The greater the need, the more quickly does use come to our aid.

The Boers were not in strength greater than our own, and as the ground sloped away behind us, we were able to detach two troops unseen by the enemy. These arrived in twenty minutes at his rear, and his horses being thus threatened he retreated hastily. We had suffered a few casualties, but had none killed; our scout escaped with the loss of his horse and with flesh wounds.

Some weeks later I had an adventure not unlike his. It must have been equally interesting to the spectators – the spectator, I should say, for there was only one besides the marksmen. I was riding to the township of Molteno with a despatch for the commandant, and after descending a hillside I heard a shot. Looking over my shoulder I saw a party of Boers upon the sky-line, some mounted and others in the act of dismounting. They were about four hundred yards from me, a nice, sporting range. To my left was a farm with a neat stone wall about it, enclosing, on my side, an orchard. I was riding Tim, and I instantly gave him the spurs and bent low over his neck. As I flashed by the gate of the orchard, accompanied by a hot fusillade, I saw a girl standing in its gateway. Her pretty face was framed in a big Dutch sun-bonnet; she was far enough from the line of fire to be safe; and her expression was of mild interest. I was a rooinek; I was not personally known to her; and she was not concerned about me. I shall never forget the expression of that girl's face. I might have been a fleeing springbok.

I had served nearly six months with the Q.M.I. when word arrived that we were to be disbanded, owing to a decision to reorganize the Cape Defence Force. I was sorry. I had to part with Tim and with many good comrades.

I went to East London, spent my pay, and enlisted in Damant's Horse.

§ 3

I have little to tell of my service with that regiment. Peace came five months after my enlistment, and three of those months were spent in hospital with intermittent fever. Possibly my illness saved my life, for the regiment was twice cut up during my absence. Colonel Damant, in private life a detective, was a man of lion-like courage and too little caution. Fit to lead cavalry, he was not the man for guerilla warfare. From the ranks he had risen to command of a column of which his regiment was part, and was given the D.S.O. and returned to his lower command at the same time. But the D.S.O. was a badge of distinction at that period. It did not 'come up with the rations.'

Leaving hospital I rejoined my squadron in time to take part in the last 'drive.' We then encamped at Klerksdorp, in the Orange Free State, where numerous other mounted units lay with us, and for several weeks we had practically nothing to do. The peace *pourparlers* were going forward. Here in mid-winter, on the high veldt, the weather was bitterly cold, and the cavalry cloaks which we used as coverlets were often so stiff with frost in the morning that it was possible to stand them upright. The men had lately been paid, and liquor being hardly obtainable (except by members of the quarter-guard, who invariably raided the rum cask) all had money. As a means of spending it, gambling was the sole alternative to drinking, and gambling of every description flourished among us. Its favourite forms were the Crown and Anchor board and the game of two-up. There were of course the sharps and the mugs, and many of the former raked in hundreds. I have seen a hundred pounds hang on the toss of a penny. At night the lamp-lit Crown and Anchor boards, pitched in the open lines, were thronged by eager players and interested spectators. It was an evening's entertainment to stroll through the dark lines from board to board, and study the faces which the lamps threw into relief against the night. There was excitement too, and the high play resulted in some tragedies. Our farrier-sergeant attempted, and another man accomplished, suicide. I myself lost twenty pounds in ten minutes, and stopped because I had only a pound remaining. Many commanding officers countenanced gambling, for the reason that it led men to re-enlist.

The day came when the bugles blew Retreat, to notify the war's end; and I recall one scene which closely followed that. From over the veldt one morning came a dark column, heading towards our camp. We all turned out to see what was approaching us. It was a big Boer commando, under a slender escort. We watched them as they rode by, and all were well-mounted and fairly clothed and looked in the best of spirits. For quality and condition our horses were not to be classed with theirs; in all our lines we could not have shown a dozen to compare with them. And every Boer, without exception, carried one of our cavalry cloaks on the front of his saddle! Gallantly those burghers cantered by, less like prisoners than like the van of a victorious army. This was one of the first surrenders under the peace terms.

We then trekked to Kimberley, where the regiment, originally Remington's Guides, was raised, but before we arrived there I fell ill again, and made the last part of the journey on a wagon. For days I had been ill, but our doctor chose to believe that I was malingering, and refused me either quinine or a place in the ambulance. However, upon our reaching Kimberley, my condition so alarmed him, that, fearing I had enteric and might die on his hands, he rushed me off in his cart to the base hospital, and got me admitted. With medical treatment I soon recovered, and was fit to go out in a fortnight.

I was given a railway warrant, and travelling in an open truck to Cape Town, had sight of the old castle on the third day. I had never seen Cape Town before and was pleased to be there.

CHAPTER III

*

I HAD to go to the castle for my discharge, and there I received a month's pay that was owing to me. This, a matter of seven pounds odd, was all I had now, though I afterwards drew an additional five for 'blood' money. The war being over, I could not, as before, walk up to a recruiting-office and solve my financial difficulties; and I saw that the great number of disbanded soldiers must create a glut in the labour market. However, I was far from gloomy about my prospects. I still rejoiced in my freedom and trusted my luck. Moreover, the novelty and quaintness of Cape Town amused me. As I walked its streets I revelled in new sensations; and, visibly an adventurer in the world, I knew the adventurer's joy.

I found lodgings at first above a fruiterer's shop, and made hardly a pretence of looking for work until I was down to my last pound. I then went to the docks, where discharged soldiers were being employed as stevedores.

Here the work was light and the wages in proportion. Five shillings a day was our reward, which was a shilling more than the wages of a kaffir; but this scheme, of employing white instead of black labour, was merely a temporary expedient to give work to the idle. We pushed trucks about with small loads on them: in fact, we played at wharf-labouring, our numbers being much in excess of those required. Our operations were confined to loading transports and were directed by A.S.C. men; and when

there was no ship to load we loafed. Even then some mur-
mured against their lot. My sole difficulty was to make
both ends meet, and I soon found it impossible to feed
decently and pay the rent of my room. A fellow-worker
suggested the Salvation Army. I was rather shocked at the
notion, but he told me that he was staying at their barracks
and the accommodation was tolerable. So I went with him
that evening and paid for my lodging there. I slept in a
large dormitory, like a barrack-room, where the beds were
clean and the company unobjectionable. The saving of
expense enabled me to feed myself much better and have
a little money to spare for luxuries.

I met several queer characters here, but the most mem-
orable was a doctor, who was never drunk but always half-
seas over, and lived, while I knew him, entirely by begging.
He must have been a heavy tax on the local physicians.
Though fifty years of age, he had served as a mounted man
during most of the war, and his constitution and spirit were
of equal hardiness. He had long been parted from his dip-
lomas. As a borrower he was difficult to withstand, and no
loan was too small for him. He had that sudden, careless
method of approach which sends the hand involuntarily
into the pocket. His clothes were shabby and beer-stained;
he had usually a white stubble on his chin, but he bore himself with an emphatically West End air. He told me that
he had once been attached to His Majesty's Household
Cavalry, and I did not disbelieve the statement. In fact, as
one knocks about the world, one sees less and less reason to
disbelieve extraordinary stories. In the case of the *déclassé*,

the extraordinary really becomes the normal. I have met men from Harrow and Eton who not only looked but spoke like street-corner loafers.

There was another man, a B.A. of Aberdeen, a poor weak gentle creature who had once been a librarian. He was young, and spoke sometimes of his mother, who, like many Scottish parents, had toiled and saved to send him to the university. Harmless and amiable, he appeared to have drifted downward through no vice. He was such another as Herrick in *The Ebb Tide*.

The man who had introduced me to the Salvation Army was an old B.S.A. policeman, who had been through the Matabele war and rebellion. He was never tired of expatiating on the joys of a policeman's life in Rhodesia, and was full of regrets at having left the Force. He was too old now to rejoin it, and having neither trade nor special abilities, he regarded the future darkly. He, like Hammond, had been a sergeant, but he had not Hammond's light-hearted way with the world. In Rhodesia he had realized a dream and allowed it to escape him: that was not the burden of his lamentation, but it was, I guessed, the burden of his thought.

His talk fired me with desires to join the British South Africa (the Chartered Company's) Police, which in those days had a romantic fame in South Africa. But to do so I must go to Bulawayo, and I saw no means of getting there. Bulawayo lies twelve hundred miles from Cape Town, which was rather far to walk – though Hammond had walked it. But one morning my friend told me

46

that last night in Adderley Street he had seen the beloved blue tunic and Bedford cords; and investigating the phenomenon, had discovered a sergeant-major of his acquaintance. The latter was in Cape Town on recruiting duty; and if I wished to join, here was my chance.

I jumped at it; and that evening drew my five shillings from the pay-clerk for the last time.

Next morning I presented myself at the office which the sergeant-major was occupying; and after a short conversation with him was sent with a note to the doctor.

I was nervous during the medical examination, fearful lest I should not pass. Passing medical tests for war service was not a difficult matter; to get into a crack police corps very well might be; and the doctor was ominously silent when he had done with me. I felt that I must know my fate at once.

'Have I passed?' I asked him as he sat down to write.

He laughed, at my evident anxiety, and told me that I was sound and filled all requirements. I returned to the recruiting-office on winged feet; was sworn in, and told to be at the railway station at eight o'clock the next night. The pay was five shillings a day with everything found; the term of service two years.

I was proud of my success, and proud to be a member of a distinguished corps. The sergeant-major, a tall, agreeable fellow, obviously a gentleman, made a very handsome figure in his uniform, which consisted of the said blue tunic and Bedford cords, white strappings, brass buttons, blue puttees, and a fawn-coloured hat turned up

47

on one side and bound with a russet puggaree. While allowing that the sergeant-major filled a uniform better than I could hope to do, I rather fancied myself in this rig-out.

We were a company of eight going to Bulawayo, and with one of the recruits, a ship's engineer, I soon struck up an acquaintance. He was, of course, a Scot; I never met a ship's engineer who was not. Another was a West Australian stockman, a very quiet likeable lad; two others were tailor's apprentices from Whitechapel; a fifth was the son of a Cape Town solicitor; so it will be seen that we were a mixed lot. All had served in the war, in English, South African or Australian units; the tailors, who were not the pick of the bunch, having graced the Imperial Yeomanry. We occupied two compartments of a corridor carriage, and for the first couple of days I enjoyed the journey. After that it became irksome, though the scenes were strange. Entering Rhodesia, we came into a level, wooded country, markedly different in character from the bare, far-ranging veldt.

All were glad when at evening of the fourth day we ran into Bulawayo. I had been placed in charge of the party, and I gave up my command to a sergeant who met us on the platform. Our baggage was put on a cart and we were marched to barracks.

I was not now quite so bucked about myself. Bula-wayo and the B.S.A. Police had looked splendid in the distance; but I had one or two qualms as I faced the reality. Barrack squares and drill and riding-school;

stables and guard-mounting, and the insolence of non-commissioned officers; these loomed large among the things I saw before me. It was going to be, I knew, a very different kind of soldiering from that I had known; and the discipline in particular I expected to feel. Nominally a police force, this was really a military force performing police duty. At headquarters, my friend of the docks had told me, the routine was that of a British cavalry regiment.

We were taken to a corrugated iron mess-room, where a supper of tinned beef and bread was served to us, with tea to wash it down. Some sergeants lounged in while we were eating, and having surveyed us, exchanged some audible comments. It was clear that they considered us a scratch lot, not up to the standard. I felt abashed at the time, but recruits and reinforcements, I have learned since, never come up to the standard; and this is a law of general application.

§ 2

Being fairly quick at drill, I had few of those troubles of the awkward squad which embitter the early days of many recruits. The barracks, or camp, as they were commonly called, were healthily situated on a hill overlooking the town; the huts and offices enclosed the big parade-ground; and beyond it, at one end, were the sergeants' mess, the stables and the manège. Riding-school was in the hour between the early morning parade and breakfast.

I had fondly imagined that I had little more to learn

49

in the way of horsemanship, but I quickly discovered my error. Riding in a saddle with crossed stirrups was a totally new thing to me, and turning about on the back of a moving horse was a trick which I had never thought of attempting. It sounds like a mere circus trick, but the design of it was to give balance. Another difficult performance was vaulting into the saddle while the horse was moving. Our instructor was patient and only occasionally moved to ribaldry by our agonized endeavours, but the colonel, who came down to see us one morning, nearly fell off his saddle with laughter. We must all have been comic as we bumped round the ring with drawn faces and painfully stiffened shoulders, but one of the tailors was a side-splitter. The simile of the monkey on a stick conveys no idea of the picture he presented as he trotted with crossed stirrups. Next to him in comic order was the Scotch engineer, who was aided by nature in being round-shouldered. The Australian was a very fine rider and did most of the horse-breaking afterwards, but he too was amusing in his efforts to acquire the cavalry seat. Acquired, it was not of much use to us, for, except on ceremonial parades, no one rode in the cavalry style. Once away from headquarters it was quite forgotten.

On the day I received my blue tunic and overalls from the regimental tailor I was as pleased as a débutante with her Court dress, and I made it my business to give them an immediate airing. A fellow-recruit and I set out for town. Bulawayo was then a well-laid-out but very unlovely city of broad, treeless streets and single- and double-

storied buildings of wood and iron. Our first visit was to
a hotel, which, twirling our whalebone whips, we entered
in great style. Drinks cost a shilling in Bulawayo and
sixpence in the canteen, so we were not proposing to be
lavish; but in this hotel there were barmaids, and we could
do no less than treat the girls to a sight of us.

My companion had a rather good opinion of himself,
his uncle being the colonel of the Salisbury division: he
was a neat, dapper little fellow, somewhat shorter than I.
We ordered whisky and succeeded in sequestering the
attention of the prettier of the two barmaids. It was
afternoon and the bar was almost empty. Although the
hour was far from lighting-up time, it presently occurred
to her (wise virgin) that a lamp was in need of trimming.
She came out from behind the bar and mounted a high
stool to trim the lamp; and when this was done she betrayed a pretty hesitancy. She was little; the stool was
high: how was she to get down? My companion sprang
to assist her; but, as I have observed, he was lacking in
inches.

It was a sharp set-back for my poor friend, but perhaps
he was none the worse for it. I lowered her from the
stool; and we had another drink, at the expense of the
house. I became a regular customer at that hotel.

Of the personnel of the force I found that a large
proportion were public-school men. This, from my
acquaintance with the Cape Mounted Rifles, did not surprise me. Many had held commissions in the Army or in
the Militia, and generally were men of a very good stamp.

The yeoman-farmer element was noticeable; and the rest were as mixed a set as my fellow-recruits. Until the war the force had been entirely recruited in England, and practically all were of British extraction. The Colonial Dutch had no taste at all for mounted-police work, which was rather to the advantage of South Africa, as it was the means of introducing the best British stock.

Dismissed from 'the square' and from riding-school, it was not very long before I developed a wish for a change. Depôt life, with its round of guards, parades and morning and evening stables; the polishing of saddles till you could see your face in them; the burnishing of bits, spurs, buttons and even of heel-plates (not, at least, of stable-forks, as in a certain regiment of the British cavalry) grew monotonous and tiresome. There was one small bit of excitement, when a mob tried to lynch a kaffir prisoner and we had to guard the gaol; and I had one welcome holiday from camp when I went with an officer's patrol-party which had to make a tour of a district supposed to be disaffected. The country was wilder than anything I had ever seen; mostly forest and of a great and varied beauty. There were very few white settlers here. Once we came to an Englishman's farm where two smiling girls, his daughters, brought coffee out to us. More thoroughly English girls I have never seen, and it was strange to think of them living here, isolated, among a population of savages, whose mutterings were then giving the authorities uneasiness. They must well have known their danger, and their brave looks compelled one's admiration.

After this holiday, depôt life had even less of charm for me, and I made application for transfer to an out-station. Rinderpest was raging at this time, and I was sent to a small guard-post twenty miles away. A corporal and three men were stationed here. Our duties were to patrol the surrounding country, making contact with the next post, and see that no cattle were moved without a permit. We lived in bell-tents and kept our horses in a thorn en-closure or kraal. The enclosure was to protect them against lions, of which there were many in the district. We in our tents were unprotected; but it is said that a lion will eat a donkey before a horse, a horse before an ox, an ox before a kaffir, and a kaffir before a white man; so, theoretically, as we had horse-boys, we were safe enough. A few donkeys and bullocks would have made us safer, but I don't recollect being more than occasionally uneasy.

A man at Victoria Falls, waking one night, had the nasty experience of seeing a lion's head in his tent door; but the beast, it appeared, was merely curious, for he retired without molesting him. Another man I heard of had to spend a night in a tree while a lion, at the foot, made a meal of his horse. Known cases of death from lions were rare, but sometimes men disappeared in the bush and were never accounted for.

Game of all sorts abounded at the guard-post, and the buck we shot made a welcome variation in our diet. A steak of sable antelope is beyond the juiciest beef-steak ever cut, though it often masquerades as such in the out-season, without deceiving anybody. Our camp was by a stream and we often saw the spoor of large beasts here; but they never came on any night when we waited for them. The corporal had little to do but shoot, and he had a weird habit of stalking the bush at night with a lantern made fast to the top of his head. The light attracted the animals, who paused to look at it, and if they came within its rays he shot them. But usually they did not venture so far: at least so I judged, as his night expeditions were seldom successful. He was an old Westminster boy, the son of a well-known doctor.

I was very well pleased to be here. The forest scenery was entrancing, and the solitary riding thoroughly suited me. The roads were for the most part sandy tracks, better for riding than walking. The vegetation was everywhere luxuriant, and the soil must have been extraordinarily rich, for I rode through places where the grass was above my head. Except for a few kaffir kraals the country in our neighbourhood was uninhabited.

One day one of us caught an escaped murderer of whom we had had warning. He was a native of the district and was expected to make his way here from the Bulawayo gaol. Our man saw him skulking in the bush, jumped from his horse and tackled him. The struggle nearly resulted in a second murder, but the trooper at last got the upper hand and brought his captive to camp. It was my turn for duty, so in the morning, with the prisoner handcuffed to my stirrup-iron, I started for Bulawayo. He was foot-sore, and I did not reach there till late in the day. I reported myself at the orderly-room, and was told to deliver my man at the gaol, ascertain when he was to come before the court, and return to my post in the morning.

I had been away three months and was consequently not loth to spend the night here. Relieved of my charge, I groomed and fed my horse, and set out for the town. It was my full intention, when I started, to be back before tattoo; but alas! there is a long road paved with such intentions.

Lights Out had sounded before I was back, and I learned from the corporal of the guard that I had been reported absent. I went to bed, hoping for the best. If I could get my horse out early in the morning, and slip unobserved from camp, it was likely that my offence would be overlooked. To recall me from a post twenty miles away to be tried for being ten minutes late would seem rather foolish policy; and my name would in all probability never go in to the office.

I was up betimes and saddled my horse; mounted him and was riding out of the stable yard, when the orderly-sergeant stopped me.

I told him that I was under orders to return; but he would have none of that story, and warned me for 'office.'

The result was seven days' confinement to barracks and removal from my post, a sufficiently sharp sentence, in the circumstances; but I had been before the colonel for the same offence on two previous occasions. In fact, all through my soldiering, Absent Without Leave was a weakness of mine. It came even to be called a habit.

However, I had not deeply to regret this occurrence. My period of C.B. had not long ended when a draft was required for Gwelo, and my troop-sergeant-major was good enough to put my name down for it. Gwelo was an out-station a hundred and twenty miles from Bulawayo, with a good reputation.

I waited anxiously for definite orders. In a few days they came, and I went with the draft.

CHAPTER IV

★

§ I

GWELO is on the main line to the Zambesi, and we landed there at sunrise after a night in the train.

My stay here was short, and I was not sorry, for neither the camp nor the town enraptured me. They were Bulawayo and the depôt camp on a small scale. I have called Gwelo an out-station, but it was really the headquarters of a troop, with a captain in command and a sergeant-major under him. The sergeant-major, by an odd coincidence, had been a brother-officer of an uncle of mine in Burmah, and remembered him very well. He (the S.M.) had been in the Jameson Raid, as had most of the old hands in the B.S.A. Police.

In less than a week I had orders to proceed to Selukwe, a small mining township thirty miles away. I was to make the journey on foot, with a small cart-load of supplies and a native driver. The railway had not yet reached Selukwe, though it was in course of construction thither.

I was not displeased at the orders. Selukwe promised real out-station life.

I was two days and two nights on the road, the cart being heavily loaded and the country hilly, and came to Selukwe early on a bright morning. Entry was through a poort or narrow gap in the hills, which widened into a valley where the township lay. It was the usual straggling collection of iron-roofed houses, but the loveliness of its surroundings redeemed it from ugliness, and I was at once charmed with the place. The valley was small, its well-wooded sides not very high: there was nothing of grandeur about it, but an air of seclusion and cosiness. Grand scenery, I have found, is very hard to live with; and extensive scenery tires. The eye needs rest in one's place of habitation.

The police camp was at the head of the valley and approached by a gentle slope. At the back the ground fell steeply into a very much larger and deeper valley, over which at morning the clouds lay, making the peaks look like islets rising out of a white sea. The men's quarters were by far the best I had seen. They formed a right angle, the shorter arm of which consisted of the store-room and the sergeant's room; the longer arm, of the men's room. The walls were lined and varnished and fitted with mosquito-proof doors and windows. There was nothing in Bulawayo or Gwelo to compare with this. There were three adjacent out-buildings: the office, the mess-room and the canteen. Half-way down the slope to the front was the stable. Every man here had a boy, whose duties were to clean his saddle and accoutrements, assist the cook, herd the horses, and accompany him, when required, upon patrol. For this work he received ten shillings a month, which we could well afford to pay. The boy's services were worth much more. Little, however, of this slender emolument remained in his own pockets: the father came regularly to collect it.

A lieutenant commanded the station, and under him were a sergeant, a corporal and twelve men. There was not a bad 'un among them, and no man could have wished for better messmates. Three had held commissions.

Long and short patrols were our main work. The short patrols were to the mines, and were not, as a rule, very interesting. Much of the surrounding country was gold-bearing, but judging by the number of ancient workings and the poverty of present results, most of the gold had long since been extracted. There were other evidences of past colonization in the shape of stone ruins, the finest specimen of which is of course the Zimbabwe: which, by the way, though I was within eighty miles of it, I never saw. But how many Londoners have never seen the inside of the Tower.

My first long patrol was a delightful experience. We were a party of four, made up by a senior trooper and two native constables. All long patrols had to be done in company, on account of the danger of a man falling ill with fever or meeting with some accident. Malaria was rife in Rhodesia at this time, especially in the country districts. It was not of a severe kind, unless the attacks were frequently repeated, when blackwater fever was likely to be the outcome. I knew a man who had blackwater three times, but he was a rare and fortunate individual. The first bout settles, or did then settle, most people.

The Selukwe country is hilly and in places mountainous, and the first part of our way was along a narrow path skirting a precipice which dropped almost sheer to the valley at the back of our camp. Leaving it, we descended by a steep and rocky track into this valley. Baboons were

59

numerous here and made angry but harmless demonstrations. It is true, though, that they have been known to carry off native women. At the bottom we came to a plain, dotted with trees, through which ran the principal river of the district, the Tebekwe. Its waters were at present low, but it was, on account of its speed and its rocky bed, a bad river to cross in the wet season. There are various methods of crossing a river in flood: one is to hang on to the horse's tail and let him tow you over; another is to cross it beside him with one hand on his withers. If he has to swim, it is never safe to ride him, as your weight on his back may be more than he can carry. A horse that is used to crossing rivers will refuse a dangerous passage, and step with the utmost caution when the river is up to his girths.

We halted and had lunch at the river, and beyond it our way ascended. Seven miles of a gentle incline brought us to a trading-station where we were to stay the night. A stake fence surrounded it. Within were a number of clay-and-sapling huts, neatly built, with roofs of thatch. The largest of these was the store or trade-house. The rest served the purposes of the various apartments of a villa.

The man who came out to meet us was tall, upright and portly, with a gray moustache that grew slightly awry, and a pleasant, well-bred face. He gave us welcome and called a boy to take charge of our horses. We then followed him into the enclosure, and he led us to one of the further huts which was furnished as a dining-room.

He set some very special dop on the table, and a servant brought water and glasses. The hut was round, its wall about six inches thick; the thatch, which came low, nearly a foot thick. The afternoon sun was hot, but the interior of the hut was deliciously cool. There is no cooler dwelling than a properly-built hut of this description. The floor was of stamped earth.

The trader, as I already knew, was a Cambridge graduate, who had been many years in the country, and stayed out during the Matabele rebellion. In the course of it a native had come into this hut and tried to assegai him. He was, by luck, able to shoot the man. For this action he was subsequently charged with murder, improbable though this may sound. He was acquitted, of course, as no jury in the country would have convicted him; but that he should ever have been brought to trial was a grotesque outrage.

I forget what we had for dinner, but I know there was an excellent sauce made from the pea-nut, which, because I expressed my approval of it, was always an item of the menu when afterwards I dined here. The table appointments contrasted with the roughness of our mess equipment, and I noticed some very nice old silver. After dinner we chatted and smoked and attended to the dop. But I must mention a curious little incident which occurred at the conclusion of dinner. A spare, worn native woman appeared and waited in the doorway. The trader poured out a glass of the dop and gave it her. This was her evening ration.

She was his wife, under the native law. He had married her when she was young, and he considerably younger than he was now. Whenever he travelled in his wagon to Gwelo and Selukwe he took her with him. She had saved his life early in the rebellion, and I imagine that he was attached to her as a man commonly is to a faithful wife. But they were strangely mated.

At bed-time he conducted us to the guest-hut where piles of blankets were in readiness. In the morning, after breakfast, our horses were brought round and we said good-bye to him. He and I met many times afterwards and developed a mutual liking. I asked him once if he was ever lonely. He said, Never, though he liked to see people. He read and shot and attended to his business. He had been in South Africa for twenty years, and meant to leave his bones here in Rhodesia.

From this station we went a short way out of our route to call upon an employé of our late host, who was hawking — that is to say, trading from a wagon. He was out when we arrived, but his woman, a young, good-looking Tabele girl with a child, their progeny, told us that he was out shooting and would be in soon. We heard shots and presently saw him emerge from a distant thicket. I had particularly wished to meet this man because I believed that he was a relative of an intimate friend of mine in the Natal Civil Service. He approached us carrying his gun and a small buck on his shoulder. He had a thick brown beard, but his eyes and his nose were so like those of my friend that he might have been a brother.

He was a first cousin, as it turned out.

We lunched with him under the wagon-cover which he had put up for a shelter; left a bottle of dop which the trader had sent for him; inspected his license, and resumed our way.

Six months later I saw him for the last time, in Selukwe. He was feeling pretty seedy and said he was going to the hospital to see the doctor. They kept him at the hospital, and within a week he was dead, of blackwater fever.

Our patrol was a round of such visits as the two I have related, and between stations we visited kraals and took note of complaints. Trivial cases my companion judged on the spot, thereby saving the parties the trouble of taking them to the magistrate. In cases of crime the offender had of course to be arrested and either sent off with one of the native police or taken along with us. The native police, generally, were not a good lot. They were high-handed and often the cause of trouble, and we had to watch them carefully. Their idea seemed to be that, being police, they had a right to pillage the countryside. They were Matabele, and most of the people in these parts were Makalanga, a race they had raided and ravaged habitually in the past. The old fear of the Makalanga for the Matabele was shown by their present timidity and their very unobtrusive manner of living. They chose the rockiest places and those most difficult of access for their kraals, and a Makalanga village was sometimes barely distinguishable even when one was looking at it. Hard experience had taught them to efface themselves, and though self-effacement was now no longer necessary, they could not forget the lesson.

The Matabele of the district were much the wealthier and had all the better land. They drank a good deal of beer. Often we arrived at a kraal during a beer-drink, which was conducted with some ceremony. The participants would be seated in a crescent, with the chief and his headmen in the middle, usually upon stools. If we had time (and we generally had) we would join them for a few minutes, being accommodated with stools beside the chief. The calabash of beer would then be passed to us, from the chief's hands. There was a form to be observed in this matter. We did not drink; we passed back the calabash to the chief. He then drank and gave it to us again, and this time we did not refrain. There was more than mere politeness in the action of passing the calabash back to him. He drank to show that the liquor was not poisoned. There was little danger of poison; almost none. We might have seen the very vessel circulating from which we were bidden to drink; but the white man who failed in his part of the ceremony, either through neglect or ignorance, was regarded as a fool and despised accordingly. One went through the same procedure if beer was presented to him in the saddle, at the gate of the kraal.

Of the best kaffir beer one can drink quarts without disagreeable consequences. The women make it, and those who are expert brewers are highly prized.

Polygamy works well among the Bantu, but the union of May and December sometimes leads to discord.

There was a terrific hubbub at a kraal up to which we rode one day. Outside a hut a number of people were dancing about, and we heard from their midst cries of pain. Inquiring into the trouble, we discovered an elderly man half-way in and half-way out of the door of the hut. He was firmly held by a small clenched hand. That was all we could see. What had happened was that his wife of a week, enraged by blows and galled by a sense of his unfitness for her, had laid hold of him as he was leaving the hut. The door of a kaffir hut is shaped so as to admit one person stooping; the girl was alone within, every wife having, very properly, a separate hut; and unable to retreat or to advance he was completely at her mercy. Our voices induced her to release him; and we did what we could (very little, I fear) to make the peace between them.

I have said nothing of the other traders on whom we called. Two, at least, deserve mention. One had been a bank clerk in Durban; he was short-sighted and wore glasses, for which reason he was known to the natives as Four-Eyes. His passion was hunting, which means in South Africa the shooting of game. His appearance (I except his clothing) suggested a mathematical professor. He dressed in rags, but this was less from carelessness than because his addiction to sport ruined his clothes and also left him little time for trading and, consequently, money-getting. His trading indeed brought him scarcely more than enough to pay for his license; but, free to indulge his passion, he was a happy man. He lived for the most part alone, but occasionally had a woman with him. He had the eyes of an enthusiast. But he was an awful sight in his soiled rags.

The other was a well-to-do man, and the only white man I knew in Rhodesia who lived polygamously. He was a frail, lively little fellow, who had started life as a London draper's assistant. He had a flair for trade, but I should say that he lived for women. He was very frank about himself. His wives (they were two) were strapping wenches, either of whom could have laid him across her knee and spanked him, and rumour said that they did on occasion discipline him. But they made excellent beer, and kept his collection of huts tidy and clean. He was always adding to his station, being blessed or cursed, it appeared, with superfluous energy. He interested me, but I never became very friendly with him. He was too much like an impudent cock sparrow. The natives were not fond of him, considering perhaps that his domestic system was an encroachment upon their privileges.

Most of the traders had native women, who were either their wives under native law or girls obtained in the towns; but this was due to the scarcity of white women. I knew one man, of some culture, who was married to a French-woman. She had been one of the band of French prostitutes who plied their trade at the mines. She was quietly-behaved, a good housewife, and absolutely faithful to him.

By the end of a fortnight we had made our round, without sleeping once in the open. The hospitality of the traders was only natural, as they seldom saw a white man except ourselves, and we were most glad to accept it, since it saved us the trouble of carrying rations.

§ 2

Then occurred a break in my pleasant life. The railway had come to Selukwe, and it was decided that the township ought to have foot police. The Southern Rhodesian Constabulary, who policed the towns, declined to send a detachment for this duty, so we had to provide it. We were rendered almost speechless at this indignity. Troopers to be turned into village bobbies! The latest recruits were of course made the victims of the order, and I and two other unfortunates were detailed for the township. My only scrap of consolation was that the wet season was setting in, when long patrols, unless urgent, would be suspended.

Foot police were quite unnecessary, as there was never any disorder in the township; and I need not dwell on this period of tedium and humiliation.

But I must not forget one little sensation of it. A lion chased the Native Commissioner into the township one evening, and disappeared in the dusk. I, as it happened, was on night duty, and never have I spent a more apprehensive night. In the small hours the streets were totally deserted; I had only my revolver, and I saw lions everywhere. A morning or two later the spoor of a lion was seen in the main street. I was still on night duty. Some callous jests were made at my expense, but nothing worse happened to me, and no more was seen of the lion.

At the close of the wet season I made urgent application to be returned to camp, and my request was granted. It was a glad day when I started on my next patrol.

On account of the good shooting along our route, it was the custom for one of us to carry a shot-gun and the other a rifle. A revolver was all in the way of fire-arms that we were required to carry, and that had, by regulation, to be always loaded.

The long patrol became my speciality. Some men did not care for it; others scamped it; others could never get round without losing their way. Moreover I wrote pithy reports, with thoughtful observations on the state of the natives' crops and of their temper. The latter depended very much on the former, as lean crops meant lean times for them and consequent discontent, so that notes about the crops were really valuable. I heard that my reports were read with interest – perhaps my lieutenant had a sense of style – and I made them works of art, if not, I am afraid, always of strict veracity. 'Horse No. – fell slightly lame,' or words of similar import, appeared rather often. This would be followed by the remark that I thought it advisable to rest for a day, or two days, at Thingummy's station. There would usually be good shooting at Thingummy's. Our officer was very seldom on patrol and might not know that. And even if he did, he might overlook the fact, being a good fellow and aware that the work was done well. He would even make patrols for me, when I was evidently bored with life in Selukwe and inclined to shake a loose leg.

'Better send Powell out,' he would say to the sergeant. 'I think he needs a change.'

Occasionally we had to make expeditions in force. One such excursion was to a big chief living by the Tebekwe River. A poll-tax had lately been imposed, and he was refusing to pay it. We left at dawn, a dozen strong with our officer and the Native Commissioner, not perfectly sure that we should all come back. This chief was a high-stomached gentleman, the lord of several thousand spears. No Matabele were allowed to carry arms, except those who had been loyal during the rebellion, but all possessed them.

We reached the kraal before the morning mist cleared from the valley. Our arrival was not observed until we had halted, when the Native Commissioner and our officer went up alone to the kraal. We waited somewhat anxiously for half an hour, at the end of which time they came forth. The chief, whom we had orders to arrest if he still proved recalcitrant, had been overawed by our tiny show of force. But I have put that wrongly. He was not afraid of *us*: he was afraid of the inexorable power that we represented, realization of which was brought to him by our appearance.

The trouble nipped, we unsaddled and proceeded to feed our horses. I was putting the nose-bag on mine, when the man on my right, in the act of doing likewise, fell flat on his back. He lay unconscious, and we picked him up. He had had a great deal of malaria, and it now attacked him suddenly, without an instant's warning. I had never before seen a man drop with malaria in this fashion; but his was a very bad case.

Word was sent to the chief that we needed a litter and bearers; a litter was quickly made of bush material, and in it a dozen natives, working by relays, bore our man up the steep hill. It was no easy matter, as the path was extremely rough and he became delirious and tried to throw himself out. He recovered, but this was his last excursion. He was given a job as pound-master.

I had had my share of malaria but no serious bouts of it. One came after a while to think no more of it than of a cold in the head. But I was careful never to go far without quinine.

Some weeks later I was startled and grieved to learn that I was to be transferred to Gwelo. The order had originated from troop-headquarters, and it was hinted to me that I was to receive stripes. I said I did not want stripes; but protest was useless; the lieutenant expressed his regret at having to lose me, but it was not in his power to keep me. I had again to say good-bye to an excellent horse, not as wonderful as Tim, but an affectionate creature with some touching domestic habits. At meal-times he used to come to the mess-room and drink soup from a plate. He was the only horse I ever knew with a taste for soup. Vegetable soup he liked best, with plenty of chopped carrots in it.

Soon after coming, in great disgust, to Gwelo, I went on a sort of patrol that was new to me. There were two of us, as usual, and we had boys with us; the novelty was that there was only one trader upon our route. It ran through the Somabula Forest, a big tract, carrying multitudes of game of every kind. Coming up the wind on a herd of roan antelope in a glade, we rode almost on top of them before they perceived us. Dappled by the shadows of the leaves they were a most lovely sight. On this same day I saw waterbuck, springbuck, sable antelope, zebra, giraffe, wild pig, and a troop of four lions. It was like riding through an open zoological garden; or Eden, for Eden could not have been more lovely. We were not shooting, having a long march to make with tired horses. It was a rule that we never shot for sport unless the meat could be used.

At night, upon this tour, we camped in clear ground, building big fires to keep the lions away. Fire attracts lions as it does all beasts, but few lions have the hardihood to approach a big fire. Hearing them roar was a nightly occurrence, but we slept soundly in the knowledge that our boys would keep the fires burning till morning. They were denizens of the country, and familiarity does not always breed contempt. Our horses were not disturbed by the lions' voices, but on the march their violent tremors informed us whenever a lion was near. Even the proximity of a lion's skin will send a horse frantic. There were camels, employed for transport, in the Selukwe district, and we noted, as a curious fact, that the smell of a camel had the same effect on a horse as the smell of a lion.

One evening, after supper, there was nearly a fatal accident. We were camped in dense bush, having failed to find a glade with water handy. My companion and I were stretched on our blankets, smoking, and my boy was lying at my feet. We heard a noise in the bush, and I picked up my shot-gun. This gun had a very light trigger and was not a safe weapon. The firelight showed us nothing moving in the bush, but presently we heard the animal retire. I laid down my gun, rather sharply; it was still at full cock, and it went off. The charge must have passed within about three inches of my boy's head. He grinned as if it were a good joke.

But the charms of the Somabula Forest could not reconcile me to Gwelo, nor was my discontent soothed by the promise of stripes. In Selukwe we had been a happy family; here, I know not why, was none of that intimacy; and my disgust grew steadily. I disliked the camp; I disliked the town; I disliked the routine. The crowning vexation was my appointment to the post of mounted orderly. For this duty I had to dress up daily in full regimentals, with spurs and bit and stirrup-irons burnished to blind you, and ride between camp and town with letters and messages. I had even to go upon domestic errands. Utterly spoiled as I was by my life in Selukwe, not even the smiles of the captain's lady could make this tolerable. My two years' term was up, and I had not yet signed on for another period. I paraded for my discharge.

Nothing but pique was at the bottom of my sudden determination. The captain argued with me, but I was obstinate, and my request went forward. I have seldom indulged in regrets; but a day was soon to come when I was to regret this step.

My discharge duly arrived, and, in presenting it to me, the captain reminded me that if I rejoined within six months, my previous service would count, and I could expect promotion. But I had other plans.

In a new suit of clothes, which felt strangely loose, I left camp that night and entrained for Cape Town. I had little luggage, but I had in a money-belt thirty-nine or forty pounds, my deferred pay.

My intention was to go to Australia.

CHAPTER V

★

§ 1

I ARRIVED, without adventure, in Cape Town, and, without adventure there, booked a steerage passage to Sydney by one of the Lund boats. It cost me seven pounds ten. Before the ship sailed I had, however, spent half my remaining money (much of it on clothes, which I badly required, and other in paying an old debt, as I felt at this time so wealthy) so that I had little more than ten pounds when I left Cape Town.

On the voyage I made the acquaintance of an Australian engine-driver, a fat, jolly fellow, whose company I was fortunate enough to retain after I left the ship.

My first impressions of Sydney were most pleasing, and I was glad to have a man who could show me the ropes. He took me to a good boarding-house in George Street. I had ideas of seeing the bush, but first I tried to join the New South Wales Police. In this I was not successful. They wanted, for the mounted branch, Australians, or men domiciled in Australia, and they told me to come back in a year or two's time. Thinking that I should like to be a boundary-rider (a sheep or cattle station hand, who rides the boundaries, repairs fences and so on) I tried several of the agencies that swarm in Castlereagh Street, but learned that without local references no job was obtainable. My engine-driving friend had been no more successful. He had been employed on the Queensland government railways, left them to go to the Transvaal,

74

and returned for his own not very clear reasons. He could not obtain re-employment in Queensland, nor enter any other State service as a driver; times were very bad in Australia, owing to a severe drought; and he was headed off everywhere.

After three weeks of fruitless questing in Sydney we determined to make for the bush. Funds were running low; I myself was almost out of money; Mick had a pound or so left.

When we had bought blankets and billy-cans, we had about twelve shillings between us.

Our way lay over the Blue Mountains, and we took the train to Penrith, thirty miles out, a town at the foot of this range. Half-way up it was the little village of Springwood, where long afterwards I was to live, near Norman Lindsay. The month was November, and the sun hot, though the summer had hardly begun. Being more accustomed, of late, to riding than to walking, I found the going hard as we started the ascent. For Mick it was worse, for he had his fat to carry, as well as a heavy swag. There were many on the road besides us, and there seemed to be more coming down than going up, which did not augur well. In truth this was one of the worst seasons that Australia had ever experienced, and droves of men were tramping in search of work. Most had neatly-rolled swags, some with tents or waterproof wrapped round them; and the few who had none were regarded with disfavour and suspicion. The swag, among wayfarers in the bush, is the emblem of respectability: it distinguishes its carrier from the tramp and outcast. The greatest calamity on the track is to lose one's swag; and no true swagman, however pressed, will sell his. The swag says: 'I am an honest traveller, looking for work; being provided, I shall not steal; I have change of clothing, and am, therefore, fit to mix with my fellows.'

There were men of all kinds on the road: nondescripts, like myself; artisans and mechanics, like my engine-driver; city labourers and derelicts, and genuine bushmen.

Careful though we were of our money, we had none left by the time we reached Katoomba, a summer resort in the higher parts of the range. But it was necessary to eat. . . .

We ate. The butchers and the bakers were very good. How, without going bankrupt, they supported that half-starved army throughout this summer, I have often been curious to know. But they did, and were cheerful about it. Sometimes we chopped wood for the bakers, but usually there was none to chop. There were so many aspirants for the axe.

Well, on we went from Katoomba, sometimes hearing of work, never obtaining it; and at last surmounting the crest of the Blue Mountains, we began our descent to the Bathurst Plains.

We camped, I need scarcely say, in the bush, and made fires on which we boiled the billy for tea, and cooked meat when we had any. The latter we grilled, using a piece of bent fencing-wire for a gridiron. Some men carried frying-pans, but we had not thought to supply ourselves with one. Sugar was often scarce; milk was absent; but of tea we had plenty. I even tried to smoke tea. Dried gum-leaves also I tried, and a wild tobacco that grew here and there by the roadside. But the last was too expensive in matches; it burned like tinder and was ashes in a few minutes.

We broke our downward journey at Lithgow, a coal town where there were ironworks. Our services were not required anywhere here. Near the centre of the town was an abandoned foundry, then used as a camp by swagmen. There were a score or more gathered here when we arrived. And again I know not how the local butchers and bakers survived the invasion.

We stayed two days in Lithgow and I was glad to depart. The town was a sad place, and the ugliness and squalor of our camp in the old foundry depressed me. Our downhill tramp was pleasant, and pleasant our view of the plains.

We came to Bathurst, a pretty country town, and camped on its outskirts under some willows by a stream. Food was again procurable (I chopped wood here with a broken-handled axe which left my hands raw for several days) but inquiry showed that the economic problem was as far as ever from solution. My mate and I discussed the position earnestly. Which was the better to do? to go on or to go back? We were a hundred and forty miles from Sydney now. But it was not the distance that troubled us. It was the fact that we should, unless Providence intervened, arrive in Sydney penniless. Our situation might then become a great deal worse than it was at present.

Yet both of us, although we did not acknowledge it, ardently desired to return. Sydney was grown to be like a paradise from which we had been evicted: visions of it tantalized us continually.

We were still undecided, when Destiny settled the question for us. She took the form of a dapper commercial traveller, a boyhood friend of Mick's. I had just made a vain call at the local newspaper office, and we were standing rather disconsolate, in the town square, when this seraphic being descended upon us. One moment we were alone; the next I was being introduced to him; or so it seemed.

My heart rose as my eyes took in his appearance: his natty tweeds, his massive watch-chain and shining boots. I withdrew as I saw the conversation becoming private. Presently Mick rejoined me, glowing and excited, and showed me – a quid!

'All he could spare,' he explained. 'Business is rotten.'

That golden quid weighed down the scales for Sydney. We started the next morning.

Now, it will be seen that that piece of gold had to be conserved; so we set ourselves the task of walking to Sydney without spending a penny of it.

Hard though it was, it was not so hard a task as the walking out had been; for we were buoyed up by pleasing anticipations. Athirst we thought of great schooners of beer; hungry, of well-laden luncheon-counters; hot and weary, of the Moreton Bay fig-trees that shaded the green sward of the Sydney Domain.

The last stages were long ones, for we wished to arrive in the city by Christmas Eve and have our Christmas dinner there. The heat became intense, and our thirst grew till all our dreams by day were of foaming tankards: yet, with a resolution which I think is creditable to both of us, that sovereign was carried intact into the very heart of Sydney. Tremendous was the moment when it passed across the counter and we quaffed.

Beer was threepence a pint, but nothing remotely resembling excess followed. We left our swags at the railway station; fed cheaply but heartily for sixpence apiece (those were the days when food cost next to nothing), perambulated the brilliant streets till late, and sought rest in the Domain. Neither of us had ever passed a night there; it was reported to be, and was, a dangerous place, but only for those with a prosperous aspect. The moon shone; the air was very mild; and we found a soft and sheltered spot under a tree. Before we fell asleep we heard an outcry, followed by shots; there was the sound of racing feet over the grass, and a man flashed by us. Unperturbed by this event, which did not concern us, we closed our eyes and slept soundly till morning.

We then rose and washed our faces at a fountain; breakfasted frugally on tea and bread and butter, and dined heavily at twelve. It was Australian Christmas weather, hot and dry; to look for work till after the holidays was useless; so we resigned ourselves, not aversely, to rest and sauntering. After the crudity of the bush and the hard-ships we had undergone, the mere consciousness of the gay, bright city about us was both soothing and stimu-lating. It was like wallowing in a hot bath after great fatigue.

Soon after the New Year we had another and larger windfall, of three pounds, which Mick got by the simple expedient of writing to a friend who owed them to him. I had contributed nothing to the common exchequer; but that was not my fault, and did not in any degree affect our relations. We were mates, in the Australian sense, which meant that we shared our fortunes for as long as we stayed together.

This new influx of wealth did not turn our heads; we continued to sleep in the Domain, except upon wet nights, and, eschewing breakfast, we lunched at eleven o'clock at one of the bars where a hot and substantial counter-lunch was provided. One could have here a choice of fish, curry, stew or cold meat, with bread in any quantity; and the cost was threepence a head, the price of the beer. Those times are gone in Sydney; for the permanently or tem-porarily impecunious they were great days. For sixpence a day you could feed, if not like a fighting-cock, at least like an athlete in training.

Domain lodgers had all conveniences at their disposal; even to the luxury of a swimming-bath. Here one could perform one's morning toilet, and, if necessary, wash a shirt or a handkerchief, which would soon be dry in the hot sun. Our swags remained at the railway station, but, besides combs, we had razors and a pocket mirror with us, so that shaving was no difficulty. I had brown boots, and I learnt that the skin of a banana served very well for boot polish.

In the morning we used to buy a paper, and scan the advertisement columns, but we seldom saw anything to suit us. We did not grieve. The warmth of the weather was making us indolent, and Sydney's enchantment had fallen on us.

This Arcadian state of affairs was soon to end. Our money slowly dwindled, and, before it was quite expended, Mick heard of a job which he could not well refuse. He did indeed raise the excuse that his taking it would part us, but I had the sense to squash that. The job was in Tasmania, on a stationary engine; his fare was to be paid to it; and he sailed, handing over to me the remnants of the cash.

It lasted a week longer. Then I starved. I did not go entirely without food, but I had very little to eat. Early in the morning I would go to the fruit-market, to which Fiji and Queensland bananas came in cart-loads. Many of the bananas fell from the carts, and one had merely to pick them up. At midday I lined up with other derelicts, and had soup and bread at a soup-kitchen. The soup was thin, and the pieces of bread were small. I doubt if my old horse would have looked at the soup, but I was glad of it, for the bananas sickened me. Once, at the fruit-market, I earned half-a-crown by pushing a barrow. I lived well for that day and the next. Another time a kindly poultry-farmer picked me up as I sat on a seat in the park. He lunched me at a good restaurant and gave me tobacco.

I had a painful experience shortly after this. Mustering my courage, I walked into a bar at eleven o'clock. It was crowded; counter-lunch was on, and I approached the counter. I had no money, but I had seen others make free with the counter-lunch and depart. I had scarcely helped myself to a piece of corned beef when the eye of the barman fell on me.

'What's yours?' he said, rather keenly.

'I'm waiting for a friend,' I replied. 'Give you my order in a minute.'

He said nothing; he looked; then turned away to serve another customer. Many pairs of eyes examined me ruthlessly. I learned much from those glances. I learned that mankind in the pack differs little from the wolf.

Swallowing the corned meat, I departed – slowly – intent upon making a dignified exit.

But that was my last attempt on the free-lunch counter. If it had succeeded, I might have become an adept at lunching for nothing, and missed or ignored the humble employment which shortly offered itself to me.

I learned of it at the *Sydney Morning Herald* office, where the news and employment columns of the paper are posted on a board. A poultry-farmer at Roseville wanted a worker, at a weekly wage of five shillings!

Instinct told me that this was my job at last.

Roseville is on the North Shore, and to get there one had to take the ferry. I knew a way of crossing without paying the fare.

Hastening down to Circular Quay, I stood by the horse ferry. The driver of a van, seeing my intention, signalled to me; I climbed to the box of his vehicle and was taken across with him.

I had a walk of five miles before me, and was in Roseville in a little more than an hour. At the farm I found a competitor. He was a lazy-looking youth, and I did not fear him.

I showed my discharges to the farmer and was conscious that he approved me. I reciprocated the sentiment. He was a good Australian, and I liked his place, which was prettily situated in the midst of bush.

He told me he would write, and I gave my address as the General Post Office. When I left I felt tolerably certain that the job was mine.

Confirmation arrived by next morning's post, and I went out rejoicing.

§ 2

I was eight months at Roseville, and I still look back with pleasure on that period; but it has little or no history worth recording. I love sunshine and heat, the depth of blue skies and the glitter of green, and I had plenty of all that there. I worked from early morning till after sunset, not always hard but constantly. I was the hewer of wood,

83

the drawer of water and the servant of the hens. There was a mare to look after, and I drove her to the station with the boxes of eggs. The food was excellent; I had seldom to hurry, and was able to extract enjoyment from my labours. But towards the end of those eight months my enjoyment began considerably to lessen. I was offered a substantial rise of wages, but pay has never held me when I wished to go.

I had five pounds on leaving. I was bound for Queensland. I was not satisfied with my first trip into the bush. Although I had gone so far, I seemed hardly to have got outside the suburbs of Sydney. In Queensland I hoped to pass the extra-suburban limits.

I travelled by a large coaster to Brisbane; inspected that city, and went on by a smaller coaster to Bundaberg, the port of the southern sugar-cane fields. I arrived here late at night and put up at a boarding-house, and after breakfast looked around. The attractions of Bundaberg were not of a power to detain me long. Its chief industry appeared to be hotel-keeping.

I made some inquiries, and in the afternoon set out for Childers. I cannot remember how far Childers is from Bundaberg, but I did not reach it that night. I walked and walked, and at last I was walking for water. The scarcity of water in this country was a fact I had overlooked. Night came on; there was no sign of a habitation; and I still walked. I was following a track through bush that had just been burnt and in places was yet burning. The heat and the acrid smell of the ashes added to my distress, and at last, utterly done, I lay down by the path.

That was an eerie night. Parched as I was I slept fitfully, and woke to see the glimmer of fires. It was like being in the midst of a great camp. As soon as it was light I moved on, and came upon a creek (a stream) scarcely more than a hundred yards from where I had slept.

This brought me out of the bush; I was among canefields, and soon had sight of a township. It was Childers, the centre of the cane district. Here I stayed to refresh myself, and then set out for a farm where I had heard that a man was wanted. My sea journeyings had made big inroads on my five pounds, and I had very little money left now.

I arrived at the farm, where cutting was in progress. A contractor had charge of the work. He engaged me without question, and it was arranged that I should start the following morning. I had a good supper and slept well, in a tent with two other men. Having breakfasted I was handed a heavy-bladed knife with a beak-like end. I had seen knives like this on my way here, in the hands of some Indian cane-cutters who were working rather indolently. Cane-cutting had looked easy.

This had led me to regard the prospect lightly, and I set out hopefully with the gang. I was shown exactly how to cut the cane, and went to work. To cut it in the right manner was not very difficult; the difficulty, I discovered, was to cut it fast enough and to maintain the stooping posture. The cane had to be cut as near to the ground as possible, which doubled one up to an angle of ninety degrees. The handle of the knife was rough, and, because I held it too tightly, raised blood-blisters on my hands. Inside the cane-brakes the air was very close; but what troubled me most was the fact that I was left far behind by the other men. However, the contractor encouraged me.

We had a spell of ten minutes in the morning, and lunched at twelve o'clock. By lunch-time, although the blood-blisters had burst, I was conscious of nothing but my back. The rest, of an hour, did me good, and I re-attacked my task with the determination that, whatever happened, I would see the afternoon out.

I did. The acute pain in my back turned to an ache, racking, but more bearable. As against that, my hands were in a far worse state, and the handle of the knife, when I ceased work at six o'clock, was bloody. I could do no more than wash my hurts. I was pretty exhausted, but still resolute.

Morning, with its promise of fresh agony, brought an evil hour, but I breakfasted and went to work with the rest. Till mid-afternoon the day went no worse than I had expected it to go; at three o'clock we started loading the trucks that were to carry the cane away. That was well enough when the cane was at hand and the truck not yet piled high. I even found it a relief. But it was a different matter when one had to carry such loads as the others were carrying, for a distance of seventy or eighty yards, and then climb a ladder. The ladder finished me My legs simply would not ascend it.

I then had, to my shame, to carry half loads. There were smiles, and the boss frowned. I knew that, whether he sacked me or not, the end had come.

He did not sack me. I told him, at the close of the day, that I was going. He said I had better stay the night; I stayed, and departed after breakfast with my two days' wages.

I was rather dismayed. Had I known better, I should not have been: for it is notorious in the Australian bush that to work for a contractor is, for all except the strongest, a killing job. Contractors require a pace much above the ordinary, in order to make their profits; but they pay well. Had I had my first experience of cane-cutting under a farmer, I should have been broken in gradually. I thought now that I was unfit for this kind of work; and I tried for work at a cane mill. But the manager had all the hands he wanted and held out no likelihood of engaging me. Then I went back to Childers, and after further vain attempts to get employment, was penniless once more.

This, in Queensland, was no great matter; for, so that labour may circulate freely in this State of enormous area, a traveller may call at any police station and obtain rations therefrom. These consist of meat, flour, tea and sugar, and are sufficient to carry him to his destination or the next station on his way.

But I was assailed by a worse foe than destitution. I

fell ill, and knowing that I was feverish, believed at first that I had a recurrence of malaria. I called at the local hospital, where the doctor found my temperature to be normal. This was in the morning. He made it plain that he considered I was troubling him for nothing, and refused me the quinine I asked for. I tried the chemist with no better success.

For the rest of that day I was fairly well, but next morning about nine I was again feverish, and became slightly delirious. I was better on the following day, ill again the next, and so the recurrences continued. I dragged myself again to the doctor, and he told me flatly that I was shamming.

It is said that, after forty, every man is either a fool or a physician. Too often he is both. What I had, as I learned subsequently, was fever and ague, a common enough malady in Queensland.

I lay most of this time in a deserted shed, where other travellers were gathered. I could eat scarcely anything and was growing weaker. Once, in delirium, I wandered from the shed, and was brought back. On another occasion, I very distinctly remember waking, to hear a man say to another that I looked like 'snuffing it.'

I sat up. 'Don't you believe it,' I said. 'I'm not dying yet.'

I had suddenly the will to live; and I believe it was nothing but this will to live that saved me.

A man in the shed, who used to bring me water and make soup for me, advised me to go to Maryborough, if I could get there. There was a good doctor in Maryborough, he said, who was a friend to swagmen. Maryborough was on the coast, some thirty miles away. I determined to make the venture. It was life or death, and it looked like death if I stayed here. So, on one of my better mornings I set out. Having drawn my rations from Childers I could not ask for more there, but I had some food with which the men had supplied me.

I was four or five days upon the road, having to lie down whenever the fever took me and wait till the attack was past. I would then be very weak, but able to stagger on. I had my swag, which nothing would have induced me to abandon. I ate very little, and thirst nearly drove me mad at times. Yet I never lay down with the idea that I had made my final effort. It was something like a miracle that I reached Maryborough, but I never doubted that I should arrive.

I did not find the doctor over-friendly: but my call was at an inopportune hour; he was leaving his surgery. He gave me quinine and told me to lie up. I lay up in a shed upon the sports ground, and the quinine took immediate and decisive effect. In three days I was convalescent. In a week, with food inside me, I was well. Needing more food, I called on a queer character who distributed food and Bibles to all in want. He was an iron-faced graybeard, with dark, fanatical eyes and an austere manner. One might imagine that his charity was penance for some dark crime. We talked, and he told me with grim zest that he had recently given rations to a young English lord.

He prayed over me, much to my embarrassment, but I left him with a full tucker-bag.

I then set out for Brisbane, which lay rather less than two hundred miles to the south. I had had enough of the bush for the time being.

CHAPTER VI

*

§ 1

I LEFT Maryborough with a Harrow man, but before we had gone far we parted company. I was not sorry to lose him. Australia had turned him into a clod: in the bush he had found his level. He had not even the qualities of a good bushman. The occasion of our parting was my inability to proceed, through a return of the fever; and his business being important, he left me lying. The quinine was again effective, and this was my last attack of the fever and ague.

My plans were cut and dried. I was going to Brisbane to join the Royal Australian Artillery. 'Back to the Army' struck me at this juncture as a good cry.

Gympie was the only town of importance on my way, and that was only sixty miles from Maryborough. Between these two places I had some little trouble for lack of good water. Most of the water was brackish and unfit to drink. This was a bad bit of country and I was very glad to get out of it.

Gympie, I resolved, must supply me with money. I called first upon a parson, and did several days' work for him in his garden. He was a first-rate fellow, young, and showed a good deal of concern about me. Gympie is a large gold-mining town, and the director of one of the mines had been in the South African War and was a member of the parson's congregation. The latter was kind enough to write me a note to this gentleman, which he thought would procure me employment on the strength of my discharges.

It had the result desired, and for the first and (so far) the last time I worked underground in a gold-mine. The work was not so hard as I had anticipated, but it was hard enough. My employment, I had been told, could only be temporary, but that was all I wished it to be. At the end of a fortnight I resigned my job, supplied with funds for the road.

I did no more work until I was half-way between Gympie and Brisbane. I was in a country of small and rather poor farms, chiefly devoted to the growing of maize. The one I worked at was an isolated clearing in the bush, from which it had not long been wrested. The farmer was a young, rather dull man, with a young, rather pretty wife, already beginning to wilt like a plant in want of water. They had several children, shy young savages. I was employed to husk corn, and I slept in the shed where I worked. My eyes, the first morning, opened to a startling sight. Alongside me was the cornbin, and, overhanging me, the head and a foot of the neck of a very large snake.

I slithered from the side of that bin with reptilian rapidity. The snake, as much scared as I was, had retired to it. I found a strong stick, approached the bin cautiously and killed him. Upon my reporting the affair to the farmer and showing him the carcase, he informed me, without a smile, that this was a carpet-snake, a harmless and useful creature which eats mice and rats. I felt a fool, but he did not appear to think me one; he was too dull to see the joke.

I stayed here a week, husking the corn, and sometimes had the whole family to assist me. The wife was very deft at stripping the cobs; she hardly spoke; but she was not merely quiet; her manner was of one entirely subdued. What little character she might once have had the land had taken from her. She was its slave till death. Demagogues talk of tyranny, but there is no tyranny to equal that of the land.

I reached Brisbane with money, but disreputably clothed, and my first purchase of importance was a linen suit. In this I felt rehabilitated inwardly as well as outwardly. I was no longer a vagrant: I was once again a gentleman adventurer; and I walked into the barracks with a soldierly air.

Not knowing that a mounted branch existed here, I applied to join the garrison artillery, and I was glad afterwards that I had done so, as otherwise I should never have left Brisbane during my service.

Recruits were wanted, but I was not quite up to the standard. There were not enough suitable men coming forward, however, and this, with my South African record, pulled me through. But I was really too light for a garrison gunner, who should be a more than ordinarily hefty man.

I stayed in Brisbane about four months, going through my recruit course, and I liked Brisbane less than I had liked Bulawayo. The drill was much more severe, and there were few amenities; and there was a drabness, almost a squalor about the ensemble which made me very impatient of it.

While in Brisbane I absented myself for three days. The tedium, the restraints, the general distastefulness of the daily round, while they did not incite me to desert, urged me to temporary escape from it. I hold that when life becomes a bore, it is advisable to make a break in it at any cost, for the sake of one's spiritual welfare. I discovered an unguarded exit below the officers' quarters, and walked across the parade-ground one morning with my plain clothes in a parcel. Many saw me, but the thing was done so openly that no one suspected I was walking out. Besides, why should I be, when I could walk out of the main gate after four o'clock? But I had risen in a truant mood and could not wait. I changed in a sheltered spot, hid my fatigue dress among some lumber, and passed safely out of the gate.

Greatly benefited by my little holiday, I returned and received ten days' C.B., which I did with a light heart. One pays gladly for happiness.

Not very long after this I learned to my deep satisfaction that I was going to Thursday Island. Between then and my departure I had to keep the closest watch on my kit, or I should have had little to take with me. I lost my helmet, but was able at the last moment to secure that of a noted purloiner, which caused him great but well-merited inconvenience. We were a very small draft, three gunners and a corporal, but Thursday Island is manned from all parts of Australia, and Sydney and Melbourne supply the majority of its complement. We marched out early one night, and boarded our ship in the Brisbane River, and in an hour were steaming for the sea.

§ 2

I had signed on for a period of five years, with pay at the rate of half-a-crown a day, and a shilling extra in the tropics. I was now to receive my extra shilling, which brought my pay almost to an equivalent of that of the B.S.A. Police.

Our boat was a coaster which made regular voyages to Thursday Island. We had comfortable quarters, good food, and made a good passage. Most of our course was inside the Great Barrier Reef, where the sea was like a pond. Thursday Island lies fourteen hundred miles to the north of Brisbane, and is fortified because it commands the Torres Straits, Australia's northern gateway. I had heard much about this island, its heat, its mixed population, the beauty of its surroundings; and I was eager to see it. We called on our way at Cooktown, a decayed mining town, which had lost its ancient character as a whole but preserved some features of it. There was one street of importance, which led straight from the wharf, and every second house in this street was a hotel. I have never seen so many pubs in such a small area.

Thursday Island was the next port, and at daylight we entered its labyrinth of waters. Green hilly isles and reefs surround it, causing currents and making navigation difficult. The sight of these clustered isles set in calm water was the most beautiful marine vision I had yet seen. Far off, just visible, was the coast of Queensland, all but uninhabited except for wandering blacks.

A corporal whom I had known in Brisbane met us, and I saw at once from his manner that the military atmosphere was more clement here than at headquarters. There was no stiffness about him, and we had good accounts of the place before we ascended the hill. There were two main approaches to the barracks. One was by a cart road; the other by a foot-path, known as the Goat-track, which was our way of ascent.

We paraded for the sergeant-major's inspection, and were then dismissed to quarters. I felt at home already. Two years I was to stay here, and I felt I could do it.

The barracks consisted of three double-storied wooden buildings with upper and lower verandahs encompassing them. The sleeping quarters were on the upper floors, and the view from their broad galleries was such as never in my travels have I seen surpassed. Beyond the earthen parade-ground was a line of mango-trees, and over their tops was spread the panorama of sea and islands, the jetty and the pearling-fleet at its anchorage. Often the sea was like a looking-glass, and stained with every shade of blue.

The barracks were on a slope, and behind the lowest-situated of the three divisions was an unusually spacious canteen, whose verandah gave a view of our nearest neighbour, across a strait not more than four hundred yards wide. The buildings had been admirably designed for tropical service, and the comfort as well as the health of the men considered. Half-glassed double doors, which were seldom closed, took the place of windows, and divided the beds in couples; and over every bed was a mosquito-curtain. After Brisbane all this was the height of luxury.

On account of its heat, but more on account of its humidity, the climate here was trying; and for that reason drill was reduced to a minimum. Except on full-dress parades, the dress always worn was a cotton singlet and either khaki drill or white canvas trousers; with a solar topee on all occasions till sundown. Afternoon drills were rare, save when any special training had to be done, such as the annual course. There was regular gun-drill, occasional infantry drill; a guard was mounted at the main gate, and a picket at each of the forts; but most of the work was fatigue work such as road-mending, and violent exertion at this was not demanded. It kept the men in health without exhausting them. Every morning in the hot months we fell in for swimming parade, and marched down to the beach, where we had a boat-house. On returning, one could have a fresh-water shower.

The strength of the garrison was a company, under a major and two lieutenants, and, as must always be the case at a far outpost, the spirit, conduct and general discipline of the men depended almost wholly on the character of the officer commanding. Subalterns and non-commissioned officers take their cue from him, and the soldier's life is either happy or miserable in consequence.

When I arrived, things were just beginning to verge on

97

the unsatisfactory. The fault of the officer in command was not that he over-governed, but that he did not govern enough. He seldom came to the barracks. This, if he had had a good subordinate, would not have mattered much; but unfortunately an officer had come to the island who was not as tactful as he might have been; and at present we were short of a subaltern.

Discipline began to break up, and as there is nothing more contagious than a break-up of discipline, there were few individuals who were not in some degree affected by it.

It affected me; and I joined in a little 'rag.'

I entirely forget what the occasion was — some vexatious order, probably — but, anyhow, five of us left barracks and were absent from a parade.

Five being a rather large number to be absent at one time, an armed picket was sent out for us.

We were in town, enjoying ourselves, and receiving early warning of the picket's approach, avoided it. Possibly the picket was not very anxious to find us, but at any rate we played hide-and-seek with it for the rest of the afternoon.

We had a respite then. The picket returned to barracks to report its failure, and, incidentally, for tea. We were not further troubled till seven o'clock, when an excited urchin came running to us to tell us that the whole force of the garrison was marching down the Goat-track.

Naturally, we felt flattered, and determined to give our friendly hunters as long a run as possible.

To this end we separated. Thursday Island has only two important streets, but it has many minor thoroughfares and by-ways. It was ten o'clock before the last of us was caught. The sergeant-major had the honour of capturing me, having tracked me to a room in a hotel where a kindly barmaid had hidden me under the bed. It was, if I am not mistaken, her own room, and should therefore have been respected: nevertheless I was dragged from my sanctuary by the heels; and so, for me, this day of diversion ended.

The penalty of our escapade was a week's cells and fourteen days' C.B.; and because, on account of our numbers and alleged audacity, it was determined that we could not safely be kept in the guard-room, we were sent to the town gaol. The gaoler at first refused to receive us, but the military overbore him.

However, we had a not disagreeable time there. The gaoler being strongly of opinion that we should not have been sent to him, we were not allowed to work, but were given, instead, plenty of exercise, and warders used to pass tobacco to us through the gratings.

CHAPTER VII

★

§ I

COMPARED with life in Rhodesia, that of Thursday Island was placid. Diversion had to be wooed. Fishing and boating were naturally its most popular forms. There was little to shoot on the island itself, except crocodiles, and these were not common. Fishing, I have always considered, is not so much a sport as a meditation; and one can meditate without fishing. I therefore pursued boating as a pastime.

Our boat-house contained a large whaleboat, seldom officially employed, and I and some others obtained permission to use her. She was a six-oared boat, fitted with a rudder (the true whaleboat is steered with an oar) and shallow enough of draught to pass over most of the reefs and sand-banks with which the waters were studded. In this respect she was a more convenient craft for us than a sailing-boat, and more easily dislodged if she happened to ground. In her we made expeditions to all the nearer islands, and I met for the first time natives of Polynesia, who had settled in these parts. The Polynesian is a great traveller, and within certain latitudes will colonize as readily as an Englishman. Most of these men had dropped off whalers and trading vessels; made homes for themselves and planted the cocoanut; and taken wives from among the native islanders, who are a mixed breed having superior characteristics both to the Papuan and the Australian mainlander.

Seeing these idyllic places and meeting their inhabitants

gave me the idea of visiting Polynesia. I liked these Tongans, Maoris and Samoans who so curiously resembled us, and were different from any brown people I had met. They were so different that one could not class them with the rest of the brown world.

I had an opportunity to compare them with the Japanese, of whom there must have been twelve or fifteen hundred on Thursday Island. Nearly all the men were employed as divers; the rest kept gambling-saloons and boarding-houses or were carpenters and boat-builders. What struck me at once about them was that they were Orientals: that, I mean, was the salient fact, not their tinge of Europeanism: they were no more like ourselves than were the Chinese. Their processes of thought and their processes of action were the reverse of ours. The carpenters pulled the saw and the plane to them instead of pushing it from them; and this action seemed to typify their difference from us. To the Maoris and Samoans one could talk, as to a European; and their sense of humour was strong; to the Japs one could not talk and find a common ground. They were sullen, and their arrogance was that of the Prussian. They had a kind of ingenuous effrontery which was astonishing. During a visit of the Japanese squadron, which made a yearly cruise in Australian waters, two midshipmen came up to Milman's Hill (one of our two forts) while I was on picket. Disregarding me, they went straight to the 4·7-inch gun and began examining it; and they showed surprise and annoyance when I ordered them off.

Several cases of murder and suicide occurred among the divers while I was here; all sprang from the same cause and followed the same course. A man would come back from the pearling grounds to find that his girl no longer loved him; he would then shoot her and anyone in his path, and flee, pursued by the police and the friends of the murdered, and when capture became inevitable, shoot himself.

Besides the Japanese and the whites, who were in the minority, there was a mixed population of Chinese, Philippinos, Javanese, Cingalese and Straits natives. The Chinese were market-gardeners and merchants, and did much of the pearl and bêche-de-mer buying. The latter delicacy (the bêche-de-mer is a large sea-slug, known also as trepang) went to China, where it was made into soup for gourmands. All pearls were the perquisites of the diver, and thus most of them were disposed of locally. The European trading companies handled the shell.

Accidents in the pearling fleet, both above and below water, were fairly frequent. The Japanese were reckless seamen, and had a habit of making fast the main sheet, a dangerous practice anywhere, but particularly so in seas where the squall pounces without warning. A sudden violent gust, and over goes the lugger before the sheet can be freed. But to make the sheet fast saves trouble, and in spite of repeated lessons the Japs would do it. Once, when we were bathing, an upturned lugger shot in on the tide-rip with the crew clinging to her keel. The mishap had occurred in the dusk of the previous evening, and no one had seen them go over.

Accidents under water were due to three causes: sharks, the fouling of lines, and the temerity of the diver which led him to unsafe depths. The last were the commonest and either resulted in diver's paralysis or death. One man was brought up with his head jammed into his shoulders; his helmet and the weight of water had crushed him. The Japanese, who dived always in the diving-dress, had few misadventures with sharks, as the shark will more readily attack an exposed body; but I recall the case of a swimming-diver, a Straits native, who went over the side of his boat, to bob up almost immediately without his head. He must have dived straight into a shark's jaws. Shark accidents, however, were surprisingly rare, considering how these waters were infested with the brutes. Shark-fishing from the jetty was a nightly sport.

The crocodile was another danger of the sea. The North Queensland crocodile, it may not be generally known, is as much at home in salt water as in fresh. The shore at the back of Thursday Island was heavily fringed with mangroves, and these gave shelter to crocodiles, which from time to time some persevering sportsman located and shot. To kill a crocodile, you aim, when possible, not at his eye, as the story-books tell us, but at his unprotected under-part. These creatures ran to twenty feet in length, and one of them was as well known and at least as highly respected as the Government Resident. He was probably the oldest inhabitant of Thursday Island, and was believed to be of a very great age. His lair was never discovered; but he was often to be seen taking a leisurely afternoon swim between Hospital Point and the jetty. You would see his black head for a minute and then have a glimpse of his back as he rolled under, to reappear further on. Countless attempts were made to kill him, but age had made him cunning as well as bold; he never exposed himself, and his back armour was too thick to be pierced by a bullet. Shooting a crocodile from a boat, by the way, is a dangerous game, as a mortally wounded crocodile will board a boat, not to inflict injury, but because he has a dislike for dying in the water. The boat represents dry land to him, and unless the land is near, he makes straight for it; and 'the devil and the deep sea' becomes no mere figure of speech for the sportsman.

§ 2

In spite of the whaleboat excursions and occasional afternoon trips which I made in cutters, I began after a while to be conscious of a certain confinement. The island was too small, and it gave one at times the sense of being a prisoner. I was therefore interested to hear that furloughs were about to be granted. There was no regular furlough season at Thursday Island, on account of the difficulty of sending men to their homes.

Two sergeants, an artificer and three trustworthy gunners were the first to leave, and they, after some good sport on the mainland, returned without mishap. In the meantime I and a room-mate, with whom I walked nightly round the island, had been discussing a project.

It was to engage a Manilaman of our acquaintance to take us in his cutter to some of the more distant islands. Both to distribute the expense of hire, which would have been too great for us, and because neither of us was of spotless reputation, we decided to take into partnership three who were. These entered with enthusiasm into our scheme, and we then approached the Manilaman, who was willing and not rapacious. The sergeant-major shook his head when the matter was mentioned to him, and said he feared the major would put his foot on it; but we sent our application forward. The major did not put his foot on it, but he raised objections, and we had to parade before him. Knowing his weak point, his benevolence, I managed to convey to him that the supreme ambition of our lives was to make this cruise, and that the elimination of any member of the party would be a cruel blow to the rest. I also very delicately pointed out that none of us had been 'crimed' for the last six months, and that we were, therefore, technically, all good-conduct men. I think this last argument overcame him; or at least it gave his benevolence the loop-hole it sought. Permission was granted.

Preparations were eagerly instituted. We had two shot-guns; we borrowed another, and two of us took our Service rifles. Tinned and other provisions were ordered and stowed aboard the cutter, and medical comforts were not forgotten. We sailed about ten a.m. of a fine day, in a light, favourable wind.

One alone of our party knew anything about boat-sailing, but having the Manilaman and his boy with us we had not to worry about that. The skipper was a fat, good-humoured lump, a deep, rich brown in colour, of the name of Domingo. He made his living by pearling and bêche-de-mer fishing, and had a wife and a comfortable home on the island. He spoke pidgin English, swore in Spanish, and wore a small crucifix on his chest.

Our plans were to visit the islands of Badu and Mobiak, and others if we had the inclination and time. Our leave was for a fortnight. Really, we cared not where we went or what we did, provided we enjoyed ourselves in strange places.

We sighted Badu in the afternoon, and anchored there at evening. It was a high, heavily wooded island, with a golden beach and an outer zone of 'live' coral. We went ashore, and were greeted by the mamoose or chief, who wore by a string from his neck a large crescent of white metal, his badge of office. It became too dark for us to see much of the village, an extended line of huts along the shore, backed by a plantation of cocoanut-trees; but we obtained from the mamoose some fresh meat of a totally new kind. We had noted, as we drew in to our anchorage that the outside of every hut looked like a butcher's shop, and Domingo explained that they must have killed a dugong. The dugong belongs to the whale family, but is small, being not very much bigger than a porpoise; his meat is red, and we found that, stewed, it was quite palatable, and had the flavour of beef with a suspicion of pork. Domingo cooked our supper over a brazier, and we ate it upon deck in the light of the rising moon. Our day on the sea had made us sleepy, and the medical comforts having been broached and a tot of rum issued to all hands, we spread our blankets and smoked until we fell asleep in the moonlight.

Sleepy though we were, we had not an unbroken night, for Domingo snored as only a stout man can. For this reason we determined to find lodging ashore, if possible, and after some talk with the mamoose he gave us a bamboo hut. It was clean, capacious and well thatched with cocoanut-leaf, and we moved our belongings to it after breakfast. But we never slept in it. The mosquitoes made that impossible. Instead we slept by a greenwood fire outside it; the smoke was disagreeable, but it was more disagreeable to the mosquitoes and kept them away.

We spent the day in exploration. I and the companion of my walks round Thursday Island took a trip along the shore with our guns. There were snipe here, great fliers, and we shot several. We were bare-footed, and my first escape was from a death-adder, on which I missed planting my foot by about two inches. Luckily he did not move, and was killed. My next escape I shared. At the time I did not regard it as an escape or as anything at all. We came to a mangrove swamp, which our small boy guide declined to cross, for sufficient reasons. He was not bent on making a meal for a crocodile. But we plunged in, regardless. We wished to cross that swamp; we saw no crocodiles; and none, as a matter of fact, presented themselves. But I would not cross it again for a thousand pounds. I think that we were simply intoxicated with high spirits, engendered by our freedom amid novel delights; for I had no qualms whatever. A crocodile seemed no more to me than a mosquito; and probably, we said, there weren't any. I look back with awe on that splendid but insane hour of exhilaration.

We returned in time for lunch, and in the afternoon witnessed a native dance. It was one of a series of dances in a sort of harvest festival that lasted for days. The performers, men and women, formed a ring, round which they pranced, rather than danced, with comic and dramatic gestures and gesticulations. They wore head-dresses of corn and were profusely adorned with grass and leaves. The men were magnificent specimens, bigger even than the Zulus, though their muscular development was not so noticeable. They rustled their feathery trappings like enormous birds. The women made less fine a show and were far less energetic in the dance. Delight radiated from the faces of the men, they shone with sweat, and they did not cease their prancings and gyrations until compelled by exhaustion. Then another band took their places. No two dances were alike. Some were more comic than dramatic, others more dramatic than comic, and in some the comic character was entirely absent.

In a bamboo hut, raised, as were most of the native dwellings, on stilt-like piles, I made the acquaintance of a Bachelor of Arts of Oxford, while rambling through the village. He was a half-caste Javanese and remained a mystery to me. Young, almost boyish, slight, he was gracefully clad in a loin-cloth and spoke perfect English. Why he was here, what he was doing, I did not learn; he was just sufficiently explanatory to be obscurative. He belonged to Batavia, and I have an idea that civilization had wearied him, and he had come here for a holiday. But it was conceivable that his holiday might be an endless one, within the limits of this life. He was affable without saying much of importance, but his bright, smiling eyes, liquid and brown, left no doubt that he was happy. Not happy in the solid English sense, but happy as a bird is happy.

He told us about how the dugong was hunted, which was in much the same manner as the whale. You went out in a dinghy with a harpoon, and having struck and made fast to your quarry, gave him the line. The dugong, it seems, does not sound, as does the whale; for the next action was to go out on the line and haul yourself hand over hand up to the racing fish. You turned your back to him as you hauled, because to haul with your face towards him would be, at the pace he was going, to be suffocated by the water. Having reached him you despatched him with a knife. It sounded simple, if you knew the way, but we had no chance to go dugong-hunting, as none were reported in our neighbourhood either at Badu or Mobiak. The reason why a dinghy was used in preference to a canoe was that all the canoes of these people had outriggers, and a dinghy will tow better at high speed than an outrigger canoe. Herman Melville despises the dugong, but it appears that he will afford sport of a modest order.

The children of this island lived in the water. This is nearly the literal truth, for though they did, presumably, sleep upon land, I seldom saw them, awake, out of the water. At what age they enter it I cannot say; probably, as soon as they can crawl. The smallest infants swam like four-footed animals; that is to say, with the dog-stroke; from which I concluded that they were untaught. Possibly our own children are similarly gifted at the earliest age; it would be interesting to discover if this is so; but the difficulty might be to find a mother who would consent to the experiment.

After six days' stay at Badu we weighed and sailed for Mobiak. It was our intention now to proceed from there to Sabai, an island of good report.

We arrived at Mobiak before sunset, having seen that it was a low island and that the village was much smaller than that of Badu. From the sea the place was not very inviting, but we had one pleasing sight as we dropped anchor. A girl appeared and ran along the beach, swiftly and with the perfection of carriage, and her streaming hair and the marvel of her figure left an ineffaceable impression on me. My vision of her is as vivid now as then.

Here again we had to cross a belt of 'live' coral, gray and sharp and slimy, and in doing so I slipped and cut my foot. Coral is poisonous, but wounds from coral are not invariably septic; and as we had no antiseptics I had to trust to luck. Being on the sole of the foot, the cut rather inconvenienced me, and I had to wear boots to protect it.

We found the people very hospitable, and different
from the villagers of Badu. These of Mobiak, it turned
out, were a colony of mixed South Sea people; which
accounted for the long hair of the girl we had seen. They
were partly Polynesian and partly Melanesian, and showed
the widely different characteristics of these two races.
Their huts were of cane, plaited in diagonal patterns, and
such as I have never seen before or since. They made a
very handsome and neat appearance, and instead of
standing on piles were flush with the ground. We were
given an empty hut, and here we were not troubled
by mosquitoes; which was fortunate, for this night it
rained.

It rained intermittently during the next day and
throughout our stay at Mobiak. Also it blew, and
Domingo assured us that we could not make Sabai. We
had to take his word for it; but had the decision rested
with us, we would have risked the journey. The interior
of the island was marshy, and the beach, with the wind
and rain driving, became a wild and forlorn place. Yet
it was bitter-sweet, that shore – Swinburnian. We pot-
tered about and shot, disregarding the weather, and my
foot gave me less trouble than at first.

Here I just missed treading on something larger than
a death-adder, and even more deadly. This was a crocodile,
whom I disturbed in some rank grass beside a lagoon.
All I saw of him was his tail as he dived into the water.
The speed of a crocodile is astounding, unless one considers
it, as one should, in relation to the speed of a lizard.

But they look such sluggish beasts when they are at rest.

Every day we hoped that the weather would break; and we had also a romantic interest, for one of our party fell violently in love with the long-haired girl. She was a wife, and her husband was away in a lugger, but expected home shortly.

He turned up on the night before our departure, to our poor friend's horror and rage. He had all but persuaded the girl to come with him to Thursday Island. The husband was a New Hebridean, an undersized, villainous-looking individual, who treated us with civility, but confined his wife to her hut until we were gone.

This last morning broke clear. We did not grumble at that: at least we could expect fine weather for our run home. We sailed before noon with a strong wind, which gradually and then rapidly lessened. At two o'clock we were still in sight of Mobiak: a dead calm had fallen; and two hours later we had not moved. Then a very light wind caught us. We would have returned, had that been feasible, for to reach Thursday Island before night was now out of the question, but the wind was fairly astern, and too light, if we had gone about, to be of service to us.

By sunset we had not to complain of its lightness; it was freshening to a gale. Our skipper looked not very happy as night fell. The cutter was a good sea-boat and behaved admirably, but no good behaviour was proof against collision with a reef, and amid these in the darkness we had to take our chance.

There were no stars visible, but guided by his knowledge of the Straits, Domingo brought us, without accident, late at night to the lee side of Goode Island. Here we anchored till morning, and ran up to Thursday Island in serene weather.

Whether it was that love had affected him physically, or he was disturbed by the elements, I cannot say; but our Lothario had been taken ill in the night; and his condition was such, upon our arrival, that we had to send for an ambulance.

That was but the first of a chapter of accidents. My walking-partner, celebrating his safe return from a perilous voyage, was unfortunate enough to stumble into the guard-room. Another of us, about to clean his gun, found a cartridge jammed in the breech, and supposing it to be a dead one, attempted to extract it with his pocket-knife. He poked the cap, and it showed itself to be very much alive by nearly blowing his eye out. I followed him to the hospital with coral-poisoning, which had all this time been germinating in my foot.

Only one of us escaped the penalty which Fate so often levies as the price of happiness. The major, I think, did not see the matter in quite that light. He said that he might have known there would be casualties.

Early in my second year at Thursday Island I began to write prose and verse for the Sydney 'Bulletin,' and having success with my contributions, I continued them until I left. This was in the editorship of J. F. Archibald, a man of strong character, who guided Australian thought for many years. Caring not a rap what the public wanted, it came about that what they wanted was what he gave them. Other journalists, called great, have been mere panders to the public. Archibald was the public's lord.

Before my two years' term at the Island was up, and while I had yet three years' service ahead of me, I decided to buy my discharge. My journalistic earnings had not enriched me, but they had enabled me to save a bit.

In February of 1908 I went south by the steamer which had brought me here – once more a civilian.

CHAPTER VIII

★

§ 1

NEW ZEALAND was to be my next stage; and after a holiday in Sydney I took ship thither. I have used the word 'stage,' because, although I wished to see New Zealand, I regarded it primarily as a halting-place on my way to the South Seas, which I was in no hurry to reach, in an interesting world.

On arrival at Auckland I continued my holiday – being in funds – the while I deliberated upon a move. The season was autumn, the pleasantest time of year in Australasia, and the unaccustomed coolness of the climate greatly refreshed me. The Aucklanders reminded me of English people of the finest rural type, and I saw an extraordinary number of beautiful women here – beautiful with that uncommon threefold excellence of complexion, feature and figure.

I had heard of the kauri-gum fields, and they attracted me. In Auckland I was in the midst of them, and on making inquiries I learned of the existence of a place called Gumtown. Gumtown was only one of many centres of the gum-digging industry; but all were alike to me, and I plumped for Gumtown.

One reached it by sea and river; and I duly arrived, by coaster and steam-launch.

It seemed that Gumtown's affix had been misapplied. I found a hotel, a post office, two general stores and half a dozen residences. The hotel-keeper was also the postmaster, the constable and one of the store-keepers. He was really all of Gumtown that mattered, and I consulted him about my design. He painted no very rosy picture for me, but was ready enough to assist me, and I bought of him provisions, a tent, pots and pans, and various implements. When all was ready I set out, mounted on a horse, and accompanied by a guide and a string of pack-horses, for the spot that had been selected for me.

The necessity for pack-animals in place of a vehicle was soon evident, for we travelled by mountain-tracks and bridle-paths, and the country was very rough. At length, after passing a timber-getters' shanty, we came to the place where I was to camp. It would well have suited a hermit, for it was a complete solitude, but I was not displeased with it on that account, and I liked the situation. Leaving my goods upon the ground, the pack-man rode away, and I put up my tent by a rivulet, among some tree-ferns. I then made a fire-place, setting up two vertical sticks with a horizontal cross-piece; which done, I cut some firewood and cooked my supper.

My experience upon the track in Australia had made me fairly capable in these circumstances: I could cook a damper and make a baking-powder loaf, and the flap-jack, or bush pancake, was not beyond me. After supper I smoked contentedly by my fire, and was careful to cover the embers with ashes, before turning into my blankets.

My implements were an axe, a spade and a spear. The last was a slender instrument, the length of a walking-stick, with a handle similar to that of a small spade. It was for probing the ground for gum, much of which lay two or three inches below the surface. The gum being hard (the so-called amber mouthpiece of a pipe is usually of kauri gum) it could not, when struck, escape detection; and it gave a peculiar ring which the ear soon distinguished from the dead sound given by a stone. Having located the gum, and ascertained its dimensions, so as not to break it, the spade was brought into action to disinter it. The pieces varied in size from that of a pebble to lumps as big as a man's head; but these, I must add, were rare and caused great rapture. It was long before I struck gum bigger than road metal.

I had little enough luck the first day; on the second I met a timber-getter from the shanty, who put me up to some wrinkles, and told me furthermore that I should be most unwise to stay in my tent through the winter. There was an empty shanty not far away, and this he advised me to occupy. I inspected the shanty; but before I could move my things heavy rain commenced.

My flour was the risk, or I would have moved in the rain; but I had no means of transporting it save on my back, and no covering for it but sacking. The rain was torrential. I had dug a deep trench round my tent, but I might as well have scratched the earth with a pen-knife. The tent was flooded, but I saved my perishable provisions by making a staging for them. I slept in wet blankets until the rain stopped, at the end of three days.

In the shanty I was in very comfortable quarters. It

was built of slabs and roofed with large wooden shingles. There was a living-room and a sleeping-room; in the latter a rough bedstead; in the former a great open fire-place, a table, stools and cupboard. I could now look forward with equanimity to the winter, which by this time was close at hand. After a while I was joined by a cat, who came from I know not where, and I began to feel like an inland Robinson Crusoe.

The shanty stood on the high side of a clearing surrounded by tall trees, and a stream ran conveniently at the bottom of it. Thus I had wood and water within a few yards of me, and when the cold weather set in I had plenty of use for my axe. The New Zealand bush has this great advantage for the bushman, that much of its timber will burn green, on account of its resinous quality. I had had not much experience with the axe, but I quickly became handy with it, and logs as long as myself burned nightly on my fire. I know no exercise more exhilarating than that of tree-felling; every tree felled is a conquest; every log one lops from it a partition of the spoils. Tree-felling appeals to the innate savage in one, from which the deepest enjoyments of life spring.

Gum-digging, I think, makes a similar appeal, being a form of hunting. There were days when I drew blank, and days when the find could hardly be carried home. Those were great moments when, having struck a lump of gum, I probed further, found more, discovered that I was on a pocket! Then would come feverish digging, with a total unconsciousness of labour and the passage of time. Sweating and triumphant, I would regard the knobbly brown lumps laid on the bank, gleaming where the spade had struck them, and joyfully bear them home in the bag on my back. The financial gain might be a couple of pounds, but no gold-digger, unearthing a hundred-ounce nugget, could have had more pleasure and excitement.

At night, by the blazing fire, I scraped the gum. That too was a pleasure — to see the bright amber emerge from its crust of earth. All gum had to be scraped, and rescraped by the buyer, before it was marketed, and good scraping made a difference to the price one got, besides giving æsthetic satisfaction. Periodically the packman came with his team, weighed the bagged gum on a steel-yard, and took it away.

For several months I never left my clearing except to wander the hills with spade and spear. There were few diggers in my neighbourhood, and most of these were Austrians, very uncouth boors whose company I could not tolerate. My post office was the timber-getters' shanty I have mentioned. These men were New Zealanders, good-natured and obliging, but rather clannish, being natives of the district, and I saw not much of them either. My life was therefore solitary, but I enjoyed the retirement, with its opportunities for uninterrupted thought.

I worked at my leisure (except when gum was in sight) and rested when I was in the mood to rest, sometimes idling for hours on a fine day, when the blue of the sky and the green of the leaves had put their magic on me.

In the spring I made a trip to Auckland, and this was the first of several visits. Mercury Bay and other places I visited also.

An increasingly frequent desire to visit Auckland made known to me that I had skimmed the cream from solitude, and late in the summer I closed the door of my shanty for the last time. I meant to go to Wellington, the capital, and thence to the South Island; but in Gumtown I met a bush contractor who needed a timber-measurer and book-keeper, and he persuaded me that this was just the job for me. His contract was for cutting kauri timber in the neighbourhood of Mercury Bay, and thither I went with him.

Book-keeping I knew something about, but timber-measuring was new to me. However, with the aid of a ready-reckoner, which gave the cubic measurements on the simply acquired data of length and girth, I was soon up to the business; and pleasantly enough I passed the time in the bush, running the tape over the logs; and less pleasantly in the office, making up the accounts. But these occupied not many hours a week, and I had much time to myself.

My boss had a gang of sixteen, and we all lived together in a shanty similar to that I had left. It was, of course, very much bigger, and had a long table in the centre and bunks, as in a forecastle, on each side. We had a good cook, a little hunchback, and messed well, the boss presiding at the table Among the hands were two Maoris, and I taught the younger to play chess. I am not a good chess-player, but, allowing that, I had some cause for surprise when, after three games, he beat me. To show that this was no fluke, he did it again. But the Maori, like all Polynesians, is quick-witted and a ready learner. All he lacks is the white man's capacity to plod.

Being much alone with the cook when the men were out, I learned something of cooking here, and this learning was for a week put to a severe test. The cook was a racing-man and owned a horse. This statement may astonish, but it will not astonish people who know New Zealand. Desiring to see his horse run at a big meeting in Auckland, he prevailed on me to act as his locum tenens.

In a bush camp in Australia this would not have been difficult, but in New Zealand, and especially in the kauri timber country, a cook needs to be highly proficient. He must be able to make not only the best of bread, but pastry and cakes, and a variety of meat dishes.

I had a week's special tuition before this great trial, through which I passed with credit, if not with glory. There were one or two little mishaps: the tarts one day showed signs of petrifaction, and a batch of bread failed to rise to the occasion: but there were no audible complaints and not many leavings. That, however, was an act of temerity which I have never repeated. The horse, I am glad to say, won, and the whisky which his owner brought back with him smoothed all ruffled feelings.

Soon afterwards I made up my mind to leave. My

plans, as before, were to go south, and, when I had seen enough of New Zealand, to the South Seas. Some talk I had had with an old gum-digger had led me to select Tahiti as my South Sea destination. He had lived there, and he assured me that, with fifty pounds, a man might live there for ever, with the least possible exertion. His difficulty, owing to the fact that he drank, was to gather fifty pounds. While I did not propose to live there for ever, this description of the place allured me, and all that he said added to my desire to see it.

Thus, when I left the kauri timber country, I considered that I was already on my way to this most blest of islands.

§ 2

Wellington, the capital of New Zealand, did not hold me long. Cold, bleak and windy, it was not, like Sydney, a place to fall in love with. Nor had it the homely qualities of Auckland. The wind kept it too well swept and garnished; it was too much like a model home.

Frequent visits to Auckland from the timber camp had left me short of money, and this was an additional reason for leaving Wellington. I had heard of the Hawke's Bay district and its sheep-stations, with its towns of Hastings and Napier, and I took the train to Hastings. I found myself in a small but busy country town, where Maoris were almost as conspicuous as white men. It was the white man, however, who was busy. The Maoris were quite evidently rural visitors. They swaggered about, were interested in horses, and familiar with the hotels. There were many women among them: bold, black-eyed damsels and obese dames, and slight observation informed me that they were not the slaves of their men.

Idling on the main street, I learned from a fellow idler of a job that I thought might suit me, and went to see about it. The job was to poison rabbits, and the local Rabbit Inspector had it in hand. I caught him at his office.

What attracted me about this job was that it was a long one, in a place too remote for expensive jaunts to the city, and promising a cheque of fifty pounds at the end of it. This was the very sum which, according to my gum-digger acquaintance, would set me up for life in the South Seas. And even though I did not propose that end for myself, it was nice to think that, if I changed my mind, here were the means to it. The idea of setting myself up anywhere appeared fantastic, but fantasies are sometimes realized.

Unfortunately, however, this job would not be available for two months, and I told the inspector that my funds were insufficient to last out so long.

'Why not take a walk round the stations?' he said. 'You may find temporary employment, and if not, you'll be able to eat and drink.'

Interested by his suggestion, I drew particulars from him, which I need not set down here; but they were stimulating. Promising to return at the end of two months, I retired.

I shall not narrate the journey that I now made, because it would fill a volume. Instead, I will try to sketch its distinctive features. In the idiom of these parts, I took the tucker-track. It was well named, for tucker was its most notable trait. Leaving Hastings with my swag, I picked up a mate, and together we made the round of Hawke's Bay. Hundreds were doing it, either as part of a fixed scheme of life, or, as I was, to put in time. To the congenitally idle, with a taste for walking and an appetite for good food, I would recommend Hawke's Bay before all other places. The stations, opulent homesteads, were ten or twelve miles apart, and at each we sat down to a hearty supper and an equally hearty breakfast before we departed. Arriving on Saturday night we stayed over Sunday. There was no cadging for food, no slightest indignity. The entertainment of travellers was an established custom. You reported yourself to the cook or the clerk, as the case might be; the travellers' *whare*, where bunks were provided, was pointed out to you, and when the bell rang for the travellers' supper you presented yourself. I have sat down with as many as fifteen men, where there were not more than a dozen hands on the station. Rarely the cook asked us to help him – to cut wood or to wash dishes – and anyone who rendered such aid was sure of leaving the station with a full tucker-bag: perhaps a couple of pounds of the best corned beef, a loaf of bread, a currant loaf, tea and sugar, and a chunk of cake or 'brownie.'

The squatters of Hawke's Bay were wealthy men; hospitality was an article of religion with them; and its flagrant abuse did not deter them from exercising it. If fifty men had turned up at a station, they would somehow have been entertained. Many made the round of the district frequently and regularly, and the squatters knew them as well as they knew their own men.

The homesteads of these stations were many of them luxurious country houses, about which the shearing-sheds and huts congregated like small villages. Their owners led a life not unlike that of an English country gentleman. There was no hunting, but polo took its place, and they motored to Hastings and Napier and to one another's stations. Some of the properties had been acquired by marriage with the Maori, whom the British had left in ownership of the land; and thus there were half-caste squatter families in Hawke's Bay. Happily, there is no better breed than the Maori and Polynesian with which the European can mate.

At the end of the two months I returned to Hastings, to meet with a disappointment. My prospective job was postponed. Having, through a fortnight's work in a shearing-shed, more money than I had brought with me, and not feeling inclined to wander here for another month, I took a boat from Napier to Lyttelton, in the South Island. It was now about Christmas time: the harvest in the South Island was in full swing; shearing also had started there; and I hoped by one or both to make some profit.

§ 3

Lyttelton is the port of Christchurch; and Christchurch I found to be as nearly like an English county town as a Colonial town can be.

My first call was on an employment agent, who sent me to a shearing-shed. At the shed in Hawke's Bay I had been a 'picker-up,' a mere rouseabout and menial, whose duty was to pick up the fleeces as the shearers dropped them: here in Canterbury I held the superior position of wool-presser. There were two of us, and the work was hard and hot. The wool was pressed in a kind of long, up-ended wooden box, divided into halves, the top half movable. Tramping down the fleeces, we packed the bottom half, which had been first lined with a wool-sack; then swung the top half over it and continued to pack. When the whole was full we threw our weight upon a lever, which, working on a pawl, gradually forced the wool into the lower half. The next operation was to swing off the top half of the box and sew up the mouth of the sack, which was then turned out and branded.

Up near the zinc roof the heat was tremendous, and to this was added the heat of the greasy wool. I sweated till there was no more juice left in me. We worked from six in the morning till six at night, and ate six times a day, for besides breakfast, dinner and supper, there was an early breakfast, a substantial snack at ten and the same at four. Tea we had at every meal. We required all that refreshment, and the shearers, the hardest worked of all, would be dog-weary by night-time. They were paid by the hundred, and a hundred sheep a day was a poor tally for a man; a hundred and fifty, a hundred and eighty, and even two hundred, were some of the tallies.

I was here three weeks and returned to Christchurch, to revisit my agent. Before entering his office I looked in the window, where advertisements were placarded. 'Rabbit Poisoners Wanted' arrested my eye.

I still hankered to go rabbit-poisoning. The pay was less than I might earn in the harvest-field or in a shearing-shed, but rabbit-poisoning jobs, I knew, were long, and saved much waste of time and other expense.

I resolved to go. The agent had no objection to sending me, and I left that day for Hanmer, a mountain village, with a letter for the manager of St. Helens station.

Hanmer has hot springs and a hydro, but being sound in all my parts I did not explore them. I was not, in fact, long at Hanmer on this occasion. The gang, when I arrived, was laying poison for rabbits about the homestead, but we started in a few days for the high hills.

St. Helens was, for New Zealand, a large station. I cannot give its exact area, but thirty square miles would be not far out. Except for the small part on Hanmer Plains the whole of it was mountainous, and snow covered the higher parts throughout the winter. On Hanmer Plains there had been a light fall of snow just before I arrived, and this, as I have said, was midsummer; but the weather generally was as hot as English summer weather.

We walked, nine of us, including the ganger and the cook, and a packman led the way with our swags, tents and other camp material. The country was unwooded, and very diverse, picturesque and rugged. It was tranquil and noble, rather than grand; for in grandeur there is always oppressiveness, and here was none. Most of it was covered with tussocky grass, but here and there were stark steep slopes and rock-faces. It was abundantly watered with cold, clear streams. As shearing was in progress at the station, not many sheep were about.

We came in the evening to an out-station where we stayed the night; and next day at noon we reached our first camp. This was beside a stream near the top of a gully, in the high cleft of which, like coarse hair, grew a thin scrub which was to serve us as firewood. In front we looked out on a deep valley, through which ran a river, classically named the Acheron. Its companion river was the Styx; but neither had anything of the gloom attaching to their names.

Having pitched our tents we gathered loads of firewood, enough to last us during our stay in this spot. I shared a tent with the ganger and another. The former was a Dutchman, a wanderer like myself, and congenial company. His wanderings now, however, were confined to New Zealand, and he came every year to St. Helens to take charge of a gang. He was as unlike the typical Dutchman as a man could be: a bright, alert fellow, dryly humorous, and of inexhaustible spirits. He had been in the Dutch artillery and had sailed in windjammers. Of the others, one was a young barber, who had come up here for his health; a second had been a London clerk; a third was a musician and had composed an opera; a fourth was a carpenter, also here to benefit by the mountain air; and I think we had a shopman and a couple of bush-workers. The cook was what is known in the Colonies as a poisoner, and him we had to change, or the gang would have broken up.

The work was healthful and enjoyable. All day we walked the hills, laying the poison, phosphorus done up in little cubes of pollard; carrying an implement like a small mattock with which we scratched the ground, to drop on the scratch a cube. Rabbits here were in an astonishing variety of colours. The ordinary gray-brown rabbit was in the minority. Black rabbits were numerous, and there were black-and-white, brown-and-white, orange-and-white, orange-and-brown, and orange-and-black, rabbits. Cats had at one time been let loose here, and we saw many; they lived in the rabbits' burrows; some said, with the rabbits. It was even asserted that they bred with them; but no cat-rabbit, to my knowledge, was ever seen; and the difference being of genus, such a hybrid would appear to be impossible.

We moved in line when working, keeping a distance, each from each, of from twenty to forty paces; wheeling, when we had finished a strip, and turning back along it, and thus covering the terrain methodically. Not all the country was poisoned; that would have taken a twelve-month; but among those hills and valleys, jutting spurs

and crags, it needed generalship and a strong sense of
locality to cover the ground that had to be covered. Our
ganger was seldom at fault: he was both tactician and
strategist. All that the men needed for the work were
good legs, good wind and a fair nerve. Crossing bare
scarps was sometimes a ticklish business, and a man
following a sheep-track would occasionally find himself
on the face of a cliff with a drop to rocks at the bottom.
Good boots were the essential; and these had to be spec-
ially hob-nailed. They were obtainable at the station
store and in the village, and no man, whether rabbiter
or musterer, went into the hills without them.

At the end of ten days we left our first camp. In some
we stayed a week, in others a fortnight; and these frequent
changes of scene sped the time well. The quondam
clerk of London grew quite fretful if we camped for more
than a week in the one spot; but he was now a confirmed
runabout. He had carried his swag all over New Zealand.

But for occasional breaks the weather was excellent;
the sky cloudless, the air crisp, the nights chill.

The first fall of snow in the hills was the herald of
our withdrawal: to remain out longer was dangerous, as
the ways might become impassable. Later I was vividly
to realize this. For the present I accepted the fact carelessly; the packman with his string of horses came out
for us, and we tramped back to the homestead.

I had twenty-two pounds when I was paid off; and with
this in hand I determined to go straight to Tahiti. Clothes
had to be renewed and a valise bought, and I had three

weeks to wait for a ship in Auckland. To the expenditure thus entailed had to be added my fare to the North and my fare to Papeete; and so it came about that I boarded the steamer with thirty-five shillings remaining.

This was a drop from the fifty pounds I had aimed at; but I argued that I was not going to Tahiti to become a landed proprietor. I was used to impecuniosity and did not worry – much. My anxiety was just enough to salt the adventure.

CHAPTER IX

*

§ 1

THE boat was an inter-island trader, carrying a few passengers, saloon and steerage. Most of my fellows in the steerage were Chinese, who were on their way from their native land to Tahiti, where were many of their brethren. They were orderly, unobtrusive, and messed by themselves.

Our first port was Raratonga, in the Cook Group, a high-peaked island, the sight of which from the sea answered perfectly to the descriptions of South Sea writers. I felt that Stevenson's lyricism was justified, and I thought of his first landfall, so like this. On shore, where we went in launches, I was slightly disappointed. The iron-roofed settlement was so prim, so British. True, there were natives and native huts, but they seemed to have been dispossessed, to have lost their significance. I found the Raratongans jocund people, more affable than the Maoris, though indistinguishable from them in appearance. They are indeed of the same race, and speak a Maori dialect. Orange and banana groves covered the lower slopes of the hills, and their fruits, not the cocoanut, were the principal export.

We came at length to Raiatea, the first of the Society Group. Here we stepped on French soil, and the difference was marked. There was no primness, none of that air of respectability at any cost, which the English have brought to the South Seas. We moored beside a ricketty wharf, which was dignified by a port captain in white

and gold, two moustachioed gendarmes and a customs
officer. All wore tall white helmets and made a brave
appearance. The village, a higgledy-piggledy place, of
Chinamen's stores, native huts and white-walled French
cottages, was even smaller than the Raratongan capital.

We reached Tahiti so early that I was not out of my
berth until we had anchored. I was roused by a warning
to parade for medical inspection, and going on deck, saw
that we were lying in a large bay. We had entered it by a
gateway in a wall of reef, which disappeared round two
low palm-covered points.

The medical examination over, we drew in to the
wharf, where a gaily-clothed crowd was beginning to
form. Coffee was served, and I prepared to go ashore,
leaving my bag for the present.

There was now a good number of people, chiefly
women, assembled, and their many-coloured frocks gave
the wharf the appearance of a mixed flower-bed. Most of
the Europeans were dressed in white drill; the native men
in cotton shirts and trousers. The contrast which this
crowd made with any crowd I had seen was in the bright-
ness, lightness and cleanness of its apparel. There were no
gray or sombre patches. That was my first impression.
My second was of a pervasive perfume, not strong but
rather heady, which I could not name, but which reminded me of something. It was the perfume of cocoanut
oil, scented with the *tiare* flower which purges it of its
grossness. It was symbolic of Tahiti, as I now know.

Passing through the crowd, I skirted the end of the

133

quay, and came, by a line of waterfront warehouses, to the market-place. As yet I had heard no English spoken, but I had some knowledge of French, which I hoped would serve me. My sense of adventure had risen to meet the emergency. I felt actually exultant. Without friends, without means to support myself for more than a few days, in an alien land whose conditions were totally strange to me, which offered me no retreat, I was pitting my natural resources against life at its most formidable; and above all, I was in the land of my dreams.

In the market-place, which was almost surrounded by Chinese shops and cafés, I was civilly accosted by a man whose aspect puzzled me. He was not a European, nor a Tahitian, nor was he, I judged, a half-caste; and yet he had a look of all three about him. He was as light-complexioned as many white men; quite as light as myself. He smiled, and inquired if I had come by the ship; speaking a not unmelodious drawling English.

I stopped, and said I had; and he then asked, was I looking, perhaps, for lodgings?

A lodging had of course to be my first quest; and on learning this he said that he had a house, which he wanted some one to share with him. My own idea of a house was rather larger than his, and I feared that the plan might not suit me, until he explained that his house was a very small affair. It had two rooms and a verandah, and he paid five francs a week for the use of it. I could have one of the rooms for half this rent.

I went with him to view it, and we left the market

square by a street leading inland. His house was very much what I expected to see: an iron-roofed wooden shanty. It stood a little way back from the road, and was divided into two compartments, each with a door. There was no furniture whatever in the room he showed me; but it was shelter, a corner to lie down in, and I at once engaged it.

We had passed on our way a tavern, a broad-veran-dahed place standing on a corner, and thither I invited him. He said that he seldom drank, but did not object to a glass on special occasions.

I ordered bottled lager, with his approval, and we sat at a small round table in a large, cool room. A big, good-looking half-caste kept the bar, and his customers were natives, people from the ship and other white men. As in New Zealand, there appeared to be no colour bar here.

With the first French money I received I paid my land-lord a week's rent in advance. This, I think, gave him greater confidence in me, for he began to tell me about himself. His name was Edward Christian, and he was a Pitcairn Islander; a descendant of the Fletcher Christian who had led the famous mutiny of the *Bounty*. Thus was the puzzle explained. He was a specimen of a new breed, the British-Tahitian, to which successive generations had given type. The type was so clearly there, that he could not be mistaken for the first or even the second product of a mixed marriage. He had grown tired of Pitcairn, and now worked in Tahiti as a jobbing carpenter.

He showed his good nature by insisting that he must

help me carry my bag, although I assured him that it was no more than I could easily carry; so we lugged it by turns to his shanty. I had wisely brought my blankets, so that I had a bed, although a hard one. At eleven o'clock we went to breakfast, and I was taken to a Chinese restaurant, where we had a pilau of pork and rice mingled with raisins and topped with fine-cut green stuff. I liked it; but I have a catholic taste in food, and have seldom met a foreign dish that I did not like. We had afterwards cocoanut pies, shaped like jam puffs, and ended our meal with good French coffee.

Edward — Etua, the natives called him: I never at any time heard him addressed by his surname — had work to do to-morrow, and hearing this I took occasion to mention that work was what I wanted. The statement surprised him: he had thought I was a visitor upon a holiday. However, he quickly adjusted his mind to the new conception of me. He asked me what kind of work I wanted, and what I could do. I said I had no trade, but could do manual work. He seemed to think this was unsuitable for me: I ought to try the big European stores, he said. They sometimes had vacancies.

We strolled the leafy streets till two o'clock, when he guided me to the Quai du Commerce, the waterfront thoroughfare, where the big stores and the schooners were. I interviewed two managers, an American and an Englishman; neither had anything to offer me; and the Englishman was curious as to why I had come here. In fact his curiosity amounted to suspicion. I felt sure he believed that I was either an embezzler or a wife-deserter, and seeing that there was nothing to be gained by enlightening him, I left him in the dark.

Edward, who had waited for me, then hesitatingly mentioned the Travaux Publics. This, I gathered after a minute, was the Public Works Department. They were now, said Edward, preparing for the Bastille Day celebrations. Government palings were receiving their annual coats of whitewash, and the usual temporary structures were going up. Large numbers of extra workers were being engaged; and anyhow, the Travaux Publics never refused work to a needy white man.

This was glad news to me. I was not afraid of any kind of work, and had none of that fragile dignity which circumstances can injure. I could not feel that I should be any less myself as a king or as a scavenger; and to be myself was all that mattered to me. It is easy, if one will, to divest oneself, in spirit, of human circumstance.

So Edward and I pursued the beach road for a short distance, and turned to our left near the British Consulate. We then crossed the umbrageous Rue de Rivoli and entered a wide avenue. At the top of this, on the left, was the Palais de Justice; on the right, the Travaux Publics.

Edward remained without, and when I rejoined him I was an engaged man.

§ 2

Five francs a day was the wage for which I had agreed to serve the French Republic. My employment was undefined; its hours were from six till eleven, and from one till five.

This was June, mid-winter in Tahiti; day had not broken when I made my early breakfast of coffee and roll in an oil-lit Chinese café, but the air was mild and caressing. Along the Rue de Rivoli, past the cathedral and the palace of the late king, the Cercle Colonial, the Bank and many Government offices, I walked to the avenue of the Travaux Publics, with a feeling of belonging to the life about me. This sudden sense of intimacy with the place was such as I had never before experienced. I did not criticize: I loved.

I fell-in with a gang of natives in the yard: my school-boy French was just enough to win the overseer, who was surprised to hear French of any sort from an English beachcomber; and he put me in charge of a detachment. Whitewash brushes and buckets were our equipment, and he led us outside the gates and across the road. Down this side of the street were paling fences, enclosing Government property; and upon these we started our operations. A man with a water-barrel on wheels followed us to replenish the buckets.

I was quite happy. The sun rose and all about me became radiant. Passers-by looked queerly at me, but I did not care. I had a job: I had achieved my aim.

My subordinates loafed with the frankness of soldiers on fatigue, and my efforts to speed them up were unavailing. However, the overseer, who visited us periodically on his bicycle, seemed satisfied with the progress made.

Then I saw that they were not loafing. This was the Government stroke. We got on better after that. Having been in Government service I understood.

Cigarettes were smoked freely and rolled unhurriedly. The want of a match would bring a man sauntering down to me from the top of the line. At eleven o'clock we stowed our utensils within a gate, and separated to go to breakfast. My appetite had a sharp edge from my light early repast.

Three cheery young half-castes overtook me before I reached the Rue de Rivoli. They were carpenters, employed at the Travaux Publics; had noted me and wished to befriend me. I went with them to breakfast, again to a Chinaman's, and we had a good, gay meal, and drank a couple of litres of red *vin ordinaire*. They were so very hospitable that perhaps I drank rather more than my share: whitewash, at any rate, was rose-tinted for the first two hours of the afternoon.

Sunday came, and the Gallic freedom and Tahitian zest with which this day was celebrated gave me much contentment. The market-place all day was thronged with revellers, and song, to accordion accompaniments, issued from every tavern. I was struck by the beauty of the voices, the melodies and the general effect. Care or restraint there was none in the merry-making of these people; yet underlying it all was a tinge of wistfulness, poetical and fragrant as the wreaths they wore. It was clearest in the music, which affected minor keys.

Edward was still my guide, and I could have had no

better. Mainly from him, I began to get a smattering of the Tahiti language, which he spoke well, though his mother-tongue, paradoxically, was English. He knew every one in the native world, and enjoyed an enviable popularity, especially with the fairer section of it. For this reason he was constantly hard up, which was why he had wanted a sub-tenant.

I kept my gang for a fortnight, and left the Travaux Publics of my own accord, early in July. Edward had several times spoken to me of a man in the country, a planter, who wished me to come and work for him. This man, it appeared, was the son of a half-caste chief of the island, a notability who was allied by marriage to the royal house. By no means tired of Papeete or of my job, I had nevertheless a wish to see the country, and here was my opportunity. So, one morning, having previously ascertained that my services really were desired by the planter, I took my seat in the stage.

§ 3

The stage was a two-horse charabanc which carried mails and passengers, and its route was the coastal road of the island. The coastal road is the only road, and no other is needed, for Tahiti's entire population lives on the coastal belt. The cocoanut lands run up into the foot-hills, but the whole of the mountainous interior is wilderness and jungle. All along the way we were never for more than a minute out of sight of a roof. On our left we had plantations of vanilla and cocoanut, against the mountain background; on our right, the calm bright sea, sometimes close to us, sometimes seen through colonnades of palms. The reef was a black thread in the middle distance, and fishing-canoes dotted the blue surface; and here, as in Badu, amphibious children frolicked on the shore. The road ran up and down for the first part of the way, where it was cut out of the red flank of a hill. For the rest we were on the flat.

We passed through many villages and stopped frequently. From a palm-leaf hut would come a native in a *pareo*, waving a letter. This he would drop in a box at the driver's hand, and the stage would then proceed. Or the driver would shout, and a Chinaman emerge from his store and receive his morning mail. Lack of stamps was of no consequence; for the delivery of an unstamped letter one paid the driver. My fellow-passengers were two middle-aged brown ladies, buxom and melodiously talkative; two young ones, less talkative but equally melodious; a bearded Frenchman in white tunic and denim trousers; a Chinaman similarly dressed, and a cassocked priest. Everybody talked to everybody; the bearded Frenchman chaffed the ladies to their hearts' content; and the priest, perceiving that I was a foreigner, gave me his special attention. He was meagre and bright-eyed; so frail that his face was almost transparent; and his eyes made it like a lantern.

Papehui, in the district of Paea, was the place where I was to alight, and I received warning from the priest when we were approaching it. We rounded a bend of the road, opening out a large plantation. Alleys of half-grown cocoanut-trees flanked us; beyond them, to the right, one could just glimpse the sea. The driver pulled up in his horses' length at a gate, inside which was a grassy yard, many trees, glossy breadfruits among them, and a not very large bungalow.

I descended with my bag, hands were waved to me, and the vehicle shot away.

I was met by a big one-armed man in a white singlet and scarlet-and-white *pareo*. He was olive-complexioned, and about the same age as myself. I knew by the description I had had of him that this was Tauraa Salmon, who wished to employ me.

He greeted me warmly, shook hands and took me to his verandah. His wife, a comely native, whose long hair hung loose over her shoulders, rose from the floor and gave me the Tahitian welcome. She then retired indoors.

It was a cool shady place where we sat and talked. A yellow-flowered creeper, which covered the roof of the bungalow, partly screened the verandah. In front was a garden, in the centre of which a fountain splashed. I was quickly engaged, at twenty dollars a month (five francs make the French-Tahitian dollar) and we talked until the breakfast hour, which soon arrived. My employer knew Sydney; had been to school there, and afterwards spent a holiday in that city. His English and his manners were equally good, and I decided that I had landed luckily. He told me about his father and his grandfather. The latter, an ambitious trader, had founded the fortunes of the family by marrying a royal princess. His father, I already knew, was not only a personage, but was the most important native on the island. He was also, as I discovered later, a highly cultured man, with an intimate knowledge of the English and French classics. Tauraa himself was a nephew of the late Pomare and of the present deposed queen.

We breakfasted at the back of the house, under a rectangular verandah that formed two sides of a yard. Here was a lean-to kitchen and the native oven, a simple but effective contrivance, in use by the Maoris and throughout Polynesia. It consisted of a shallow circular hole in the earth, in which stones were laid upon wood embers. The food to be cooked — fish or fowl or red meat wrapped in banana-leaves, halved breadfruit, taro, yams or whatever there might be — was placed on the stones and covered with layer on layer of breadfruit-leaves strung together with bark fibre. These kept the steam from escaping and the essences of the food from evaporating, and the result was somewhat similar to that of pot-roasting. For breakfast on this particular morning we had, I remember, raw fish, which was served with a cocoanut sauce mixed with salt water; part of a young pig similarly garnished; breadfruit; *fei*, the luscious hill plantain; and a sweet made from the pounded banana and mummy-apple. The cocoanut sauce was made by first grating the cocoanut upon a toothed iron tongue affixed to a wooden horse on which the operator sat. The parings fell into a bowl until the shell was cleaned, and were then wrung in muslin saturated in water, and the gratings added to the extract. Cream for coffee could be extracted in a like manner without the addition of water, and made a rich and very delicious blend. We had cocoanut cream with our coffee every morning.

Before we had sat down, half a dozen native lads romped into the yard, and were served by an old man, the cook, under the lean-to. Tauraa's wife and two girls, her maids, had their breakfast a little apart at an end of the verandah. It was all very patriarchal.

After breakfast we went out into the plantation, Tauraa and I and the boys, and my work commenced.

CHAPTER X

★

§ 1

I HAVE heard men say that plantation work is tiresome, but mine was various enough to satisfy me. The staple product here was cocoanuts; vanilla also was grown, and there were patches of bananas, coffee and mummy-apples. I was employed in the dual capacity of overseer and special workman. Tauraa himself often superintended the labours of his boys, and I was then not required for this duty.

Much of the land had been newly planted; and the young cocoanut at first needs all the shade it can get. Year by year this has to be reduced until all shade is cut away from it. There were parts of the land where more sunlight had to be let in, and as I was a fair axeman I attended to this. I enjoyed this work particularly: looking back upon my life, I believe I have never enjoyed anything more than my axe-work in those sylvan sun-shot places. Underfoot was lush grass; overhead a thick network of foliage trellising the blue sky. The wood was moderately soft, and I had not to hurry myself. I could work in what I considered a leisurely manner and be complimented on my speed; my pipe was my companion, my thoughts enlivened me; and I had the pleasure of exercising my wits in a task demanding judgment.

While at overseeing I was less happy, I gained something by my association with the boys, in learning the Tahiti language and Tahitian ways. They were as ready to teach me as Edward had been. I found them to be a likeable set of young rascals, who could be led but were not to be driven. To get the best work out of them, one had to humour them, to jolly them, to be a 'comic.' The comic succeeds better than any other kind of man in Tahiti. Laughter is the key to the Tahitian's heart, and when you have captured his heart you may do anything with him.

Weeding, planting, gathering the nuts and making them into copra, were the tasks at which these boys were chiefly employed. Weeding was a constant job, even in the dry winter season. In the summer you could almost see the weeds grow; and lying on the ground I have fancied I heard the rustle of the pushing shoots, impatiently seeking the sun. Planting was the simplest matter. One scooped a pot-hole; set in it a nut which had begun to shoot, covered it, and left it. It might be showing no more than a green spear, or a graceful stem and leafage two feet high; you planted it, and, with ordinary luck, it grew. The nuts for the making of copra were not plucked from the trees: when they fell they were fit to gather. The method was to assemble them in heaps at convenient places, where they were split, husk and shell, with the axe, and left till the kernels had dried partially and loosened. These were then carted home, thus saving the greater labour of carrying the husks. It was next the work of the women to cut the kernels into pieces, which were laid in the sun to dry. When sufficiently dry they were copra, the raw material of cocoanut oil.

A drinking-nut (the immature green cocoanut) had to be fetched from the tree. The boy having brought it down, he slashed the top off with a bush-knife, and one drank – a draught of nectar. Drinking-nuts varied in quality, and the trees which provided the best were not degraded to the baser use of yielding copra. The boys and I saw to that.

After dinner we sat on the verandah: Tauraa and I in deck-chairs, his wife and her two handmaids on a mat, the boys around us. As a rule they had a pack of cards. Tahiti's greatest debt to America is for the game of poker. Sometimes the girls played with them: more often they had ironing or other work to do; they were skilled at making hats of black and white straw, woven in intricate patterns. They worked by the light of a lamp on the floor beside them. In picture-books and illustrated magazines all were much interested, and the pictures were often brought to me to explain. They were highly critical of European beauty and especially of the European female figure, as the fashions showed it. I could make no defence of a thing so monstrous. To Tauraa they talked freely and were answered freely, his attitude being paternal. This freedom was never abused; he was treated with respect but without servility. He was their master and of noble rank, but no social barrier separated him from them. The relationship between the Highland chief and his clansmen must have been not unlike this.

Though the outward marks of authority were unemphasized, obedience was swift, and misbehaviour drew an

147

instant reprimand. Tauraa was very much master in his own house. At a word from him the cards would be put away and singing begin. Singing, dancing and oratory are the three Tahitian arts which are still practised; oratory is falling into decay, but Tati, Tauraa's father, was a master of it. Dancing and singing, the special arts of the people, are learned from childhood, and part-singing is carefully taught. Their naturally tuneful voices made listening to these choral exercises a peculiar pleasure to me. So too were the dances which I witnessed, though these were much rarer performances. In them gesture played the chief part; it was not such as a Puritan would enjoy, but it was inexpressibly comic. In his dancing the Tahitian gives full rein to his humour and to his unashamed affection for the flesh. I should fail if I were to describe the Tahitian *hulahula*. Its action I might convey, but not its artistry and its exquisitely funny spirit. The well-known belly-dance of Africa is a gross and humourless form of it. The *hulahula* is not to be seen by everybody, as owing to the influence of the missionaries it has been prohibited. But in prohibiting it they have failed to quench the ardour for all that it expresses. The Tahitian remains in essence what he always was: a child of joy, bred by the sun upon a bounteous soil; and wistful as all joyous beings must be, through the consciousness of mortality. He thinks; he lives for the day, but he thinks of other days, which no living and no thinking can alter.

From Tauraa, as we talked in the evenings, I heard many things of interest about his people. I heard of the long war with the French, of that hopeless struggle when at last they had no weapons but stones to roll down upon their enemies. I heard of the days of missionary rule, when attendance at church was compulsory, and the penalty for absence a fine or road-work; when, incredible as it may appear, a man and woman abroad at night had to carry a lamp and keep it constantly lighted. This was to check immorality ! If, for any reason, you put your lamp out – even if it went out through want of oil – you were liable to be haled to the calaboose. Song and the use of all musical instruments were proscribed. Thus the native flute was lost. Sports also came under the ban. The missionaries collected tithes and traded: they were indeed the only traders. All this was by royal edict: they had so intrigued that they held the king in pocket.

The coming of the French put an end to this sad condition of affairs; the natives received their land again; but the valleys are still unpopulated, and native customs have never entirely been restored.

From Tauraa I heard also of the Areoi, that strange patrician society, who raised venery to a cult. They were very exclusive, and travelled about Tahiti and its neighbouring isles, giving theatrical performances and proselytizing. The qualifications for membership were beauty and noble birth, but they preached their Cyprian doctrine to the people at large. All children born among the Areoi were smothered at birth; but this practice was not urged on the multitude. Within the society promiscuous sexual intercourse was not merely permitted but enjoined, and

149

a woman who withheld herself was at once expelled. The Areoi were at their zenith when Cook arrived; but it does not seem that the people had been much influenced by them.

When the last hand of cards had been played or the last stave sung, Tauraa and his wife retired to their bedroom, the girls to theirs, the boys laid their sleeping-mats on the verandah, and I went to my own place. This was a hut across the road, where I had a bed, a table and a chair. To the bed, in the wet season, was added a mosquito-curtain, and with it I had all I required here.

On moonlight nights little was seen of the boys unless one went to the beach or the green above it, where they were in the habit of amusing themselves. On such nights the girls also disappeared. Sports were held on the beach – running and leaping matches – and the ancient game of hide-and-seek was played. If the brilliant moonlight, which showed the whole sweep of the coast as clearly as by day, did not favour the hunted, the deep thickets of overhanging *purao* gave them all the shade that was needed. Occasionally the hunted were never found, or hunter and quarry were lost: they had absconded – boy and girl. There was no fuss then, no hue and cry: the situation was accepted and perfectly understood.

Fishing was another nocturnal sport, though it partook more of the nature of a business, for in Tahiti sport is merely incidental to fishing. Dark nights were the best for this, since darkness best shows the torch which is carried in the prow of the canoe. Here I was given another illustration of how light attracts creatures. In setting the torch in the prow the Tahitian was following exactly the same principle as that which my lamp-bearing corporal in Rhodesia worked upon. A fish would come up to gape at the light, and the barbed spear would transfix him. These fishing excursions lasted till a late hour, and they too were an occasion for love-making. But love-making was not foreign to any occasion. It is the *motif* of the Tahitian song of life.

The village singing-meetings were especially conducive to it, for at them all the countryside assembled, to listen or to perform. They were held in long bamboo-walled, palm-thatched halls, and the choirs were divided into male and female voices. The meetings started usually at evening and continued sometimes till dawn, with short intervals between the items: the choristers grew weary towards the end; the children slept; but such feats were an unquestionable testimony to the Tahitian's power of endurance. Nights of the full moon were selected for them; the audience sat on the green outside, and those who had vehicles parked them by the roadside. As most of the land was divided into small holdings – Tauraa's was part of the royal estate – and there were few land-holders who had not vehicles, their numbers suggested a gala night at the opera. Vendors of water-melon and ice-cream came with their barrows and formed another line at the edge of the road. Removed from this scene and invisible, in the surrounding bush or on the neighbouring beach, were isolated pairs – the lovers. One heard some-

times the soft laughter of a girl, a laugh throaty and lan-
guorous, as the singing abruptly ceased.

§ 2

The Tahitian is a firm believer in ghosts, and I myself
came to be a half-believer in them. It was partly the
result of experience, and partly, no doubt, the effect of
this general belief upon my own mind, which had begun
to take colour from its surroundings. No Tahitian will
sleep without a light at night: the light keeps the spirits
away. I never reached this pitch of credulity, nor was I
impressed by the tales I was told of the spirits who lived
in the mountains and fell on lonely seekers of the *fei*; until
a certain day. The hardiest Tahitian would not willingly
enter the high bush after dark, and most of the *fei*-gather-
ers, who went by day, preferred to go in couples. Where
the flats ended and the hills began, the land was very rocky
and covered with a wild and dense vegetation. However,
cocoanuts would grow there, and Tauraa had an idea to
plant this portion of his land, so I went up to clear it.

There is an eeriness about the Tahitian bush which has
no parallel in Africa or Australia: one hears queer sounds,
quite unexplainable sounds: little rushes of wind when no
wind blows; the pit-a-pat of invisible creatures which
should be visible; solitary crashes in the brushwood, and
then utter silence: but I was not loth to come here day by
day, for the view over the ocean and the coastal belt was
magnificent; and I was, as you know, fond of my own
company. I had been up here a week, and the job was

nearly finished, when I stopped, in the course of a morning's work, to smoke. I heard some of the pit-a-pats and
one of the crashes. Pig, I said to myself: though why a
pig should make one crash and not another sound was
more than I could explain. Next I heard an intermittent
tapping, faint, as if from some distance, and higher up the
hill, where nothing was to be seen but an incline of vol-
canic rocks, big trees, sprawling pandanus-palms, wild
limes laden with fruit, and a tangle of creepers. I solved
this second mystery with an effort: the axe of a Chinese
charcoal-burner: though I knew of none living so high in
the wilderness. And then came a curious sound of wind;
not one of the little rushes of wind, but wind made by the
passage of something; it drew nearer; my scalp prickled; I
stared, saw nothing, and it passed by. I do not know to
this day what it was, or if it was anything at all. But the
boys had no doubt whatever that it was one of the mountain spirits. Tauraa was not so sure; he confessed to a
belief in them, while theoretically denying them, as in
duty to his English schooling bound. I finished my task
next day without any loitering. There were no more
manifestations.

§ 3

I made, of course, many acquaintances in the neighbourhood. One of the most interesting, to me, was an old
Englishman, named Robson, who had been an apprentice
in the merchant service, deserted his ship to join in the
rush to the Australian gold-fields, and from there had

come to Tahiti. He had been a trader at first, and had then married and set up as a vanilla-planter. His wife was a native, and he had a numerous, and, on the whole, satisfactory family. Certainly they brought him no more disappointment than children usually bring. His wife was a lively, spare-figured woman of fifty; his youngest child, a lad of fifteen or sixteen. Robson, in middle age, had contracted elephantiasis, and one of his legs was now enormously swollen. He could walk, though not far without distress, but was still able to attend to the culture and curing of his vanilla, of which he was one of the most successful growers on the island. Chinamen cured most of the vanilla, and cured it very badly: Robson's was the finest that went to the market. He had a comfortable house, and one great lofty room in it where he sat, usually alone, in an easy chair, with his bloated leg on a footstool.

I recall one of his stories, which was not only amusing, but cast a light on old Tahitian custom, and may be of interest to ethnologists. He had not long been married when he went on a visit to his wife's parents, who had two daughters younger than herself, living at home. What was his surprise, on retiring to rest, to be told that he might entertain himself with either of these young women! His wife corroborated this, but he did not, he told me, avail himself of the freedom, though he lost no time in eliciting the reason of it. A husband, it transpired, had certain conjugal rights over any or all of his wife's younger sisters. Thus, had Robson married the youngest of the three, two other husbands would have had rights over her.

The custom has passed into disuse, and was dying when he made acquaintance with it; so he may have been the last white man to whom the privilege was offered.

The French used to be very tender to beachcombers, and Papeete was for long the single Island capital where they were tolerated; and this was a rational attitude to adopt to them, for the beachcomber is usually harmless. His sin, in the eyes of the English, is that he is not 'respectable.'

Chief of Papeete beachcombers was Pupu, so named by the natives. Beachcombers came and went, but Pupu was permanent. He had a wife, a roof, and he earned money. It is difficult to define a beachcomber, but Pupu was one. In an almost forgotten past he had sold newspapers in the streets of San Francisco. Now those days were no more than a bad dream, which recurred if you reminded him of them.

He was a thin, spry little chap; no mean boxer, a ventriloquist and conjuror. His versatility was remarkable, for he could also sing and he could paint a house. He once tried to cook, but there he failed, and narrowly escaped being thrown overboard by the angry crew of a schooner. He was never, I believe, on any other occasion out of Tahiti, and he seldom, except on boxing tours, left town.

His vocal and ventriloquial talents were useful mainly in procuring rum. Pupu, with his ear to the floor, conversing animatedly with a bass-voiced unknown in the foundations of the tavern, was a sight that no Islander could resist; and as he drew custom, he was welcome in the taverns, with or without money. Nor were the taverns his only artistic field. In lean times, when food itself was scarce, he visited private houses. He knew well where he could score – not at the homes of the prosperous foreign merchants, but at those of the impoverished but good-natured native aristocracy.

But for long periods, extending over weeks, he would do regular work. Then there were no performances in the bar at night: he paid for his rum like a gentleman and took a drop home with him. He lived in a sort of cellar off the market square, and his wife cooked their food in a Chinaman's yard. He dressed more nattily than most beachcombers, and seldom appeared in public without his white jacket. He was on friendly terms with the police, native and French; the brigadier had a kindly regard for him; but fines have to be collected for the sake of the revenue, and so he was occasionally run in. Five francs was the price of a joy-ride to the calaboose, and as time was allowed for payment, the account was always settled.

No one, I should say, in Papeete was better known than Pupu, and no one was better liked by the general populace. The wreath-sellers seated on the kerb, the big lounging native constables, gay girls, sedate girls, sailors, supercargoes, captains, workmen, rogues and Chinamen, all had a word and a jest for Pupu. If he was not a happy man he should have been, for he was in his right environment. A Pupu selling papers in San Francisco! The idea distresses.

Unlike him in all respects but one was a man whom I will call Goddard. He was a type; and the tragic, the comic and the pathetic mingled equally in him. By a rather odd coincidence, I had known Goddard slightly at Kokstad, when he was a dashing and elegant Cape Mounted Rifleman. Well-bred and a smart soldier, he had been offered a commission in a police force, but had refused it. When I met him again he was gaunt; his elegance was gone; but he retained the unmistakable cavalry bearing. He was the ideal cut of a cavalryman – broad-shouldered, narrow-flanked, and long in the leg. When he walked you could almost hear the spurs jingling. He had had some very bad luck not long before I found him. At least, that was what he called it. He had come to Tahiti with money, part of a thousand-pounds legacy, and had handed nearly all he possessed to a bright-witted American. In return for it he had the pleasure of believing that he was part-owner of a plantation. There was no partnership deed; not even a receipt was given. Goddard was an example of what the public schools are capable of turning out. When the enterprising American had spent the money – and he spent it to very good purpose, in improving the plantation – he simply told Goddard to get out: he had had enough of his company. As soon as Goddard grasped the position he thrashed him; and this was all the satisfaction he got. He did not even stay and make himself a nuisance; nor demand wages for the work he had done. He packed up and returned to Papeete.

Since then he had been living on remittances, which he drank as fast as they reached him, except for small sums which his woman was able to save from them, and which kept him and her until the next arrived. Afterwards the remittances stopped, and Goddard was reduced to selling pea-nuts in the market-place. That must have taken some courage, as it was not like selling pea-nuts in London or in any strange place. He had been a local swell, a member of the Cercle Bougainville in his day. Of courage he had plenty, but never having learned to use his brains, it was not of much use to him.

CHAPTER XI

★

§ 1

It is possible that I might not have been so well content as I was at Papehui, but for the facilities I had of visiting Papeete, since country life is nowhere free from monotony. For me it was the pleasing burden of the tune; Papeete, the variation which kept it from wearying me.

A desire would come upon me to drink my morning coffee at the market-place, to sip wine in that cool tavern where I had gone with Edward; to buy a wreath for a girl. There were girls in the country, to be sure, but town manners differ from country manners, and each kind gains distinctly by permutation. It must have been a bore to live always in Arcadia; but how pleasant to return to it from Athens! and vice versa.

By going there not too often, Papeete was always a new joy to me. How best shall I describe this miniature city? I will take you for a ramble.

We will start at the market square, and the hour shall be six a.m., when the market crowd has gathered. We will enter that Chinese restaurant facing the hall, seat ourselves at an undraped little table, and abide the leisure of the waiter.

The shop is both restaurant and store. Half the length of it runs a counter, the shelves behind which are packed with the goods of Manchester. Two native girls, even at this early hour, are examining dress fabrics, which a stout

159

and patient Chinaman displays, spreading them on the counter. The customers are critical and hard to please; they are members of Papeete's demi-monde. Having decided at length upon a material, they haggle for five minutes about the price, playfully box the merchant's ears for impudence, and eventually buy at a figure which allows him a nice profit. Fingering the beads of his abacus he makes the reckoning; paper money is produced from a knotted handkerchief; and the girls leave, satisfied that they have got a bargain.

A third girl, indolently smoking a cigarette, receives the Chinaman's attention. She wants a bottle of scent. There is a brief, low-voiced colloquy. At the end he pinches her cheek and gives her the bottle: no money passes. The girl glances round and is departing when another need occurs to her. A packet of tobacco. This too is given, and she goes out slowly, blowing whorls of smoke through her pretty nostrils.

Two Chinese waiters, clad, like their master, in singlet and blue denim trousers, flip-flap in their loose slippers among the tables, which are almost fully occupied. Most of the coffee-drinkers are natives, the rest duck-jacketed white men. At one table is a family party: a countryman, his wife, and their three children, two girls and a small boy in knickerbockers. Their wagon is under the trees in the square, and they have come with plantation produce for the market. But the presence of the family shows that this is a jaunt as well as a business trip. This evening they will go perhaps to the theatre, and to-night they will sleep on their mats under a Chinaman's verandah or in the unclosed part of the market hall.

The waiter brings our coffee, with little tin jugs of milk, butter and half a long French roll apiece. Refreshed, we light our cigarettes and stroll out to the market.

The crowd is at its thickest; its attire as bright, its appearance as fresh as the morning. Four out of five of the people are women or girls, all of whom, Europeans and natives, are wearing the long, loose *ahu*. The fishermen's section of the hall is the most thronged, but the vegetable-sellers and the butchers are well patronized. On each side of the road before it sit Chinese market-gardeners and native women, selling oranges and mangoes, lettuces, eschallottes and Avocado pears. There is no clamour, but a low musical murmur. White men stand or weave their way among the buyers, saluting and talking with acquaintances. They have no business to transact here; they are attending the first social event of the day, and many of them attend it every day. The colour and the movement and the life act on them as a sort of eye-opener. In the taverns other men are taking other eye-openers. There one would meet Pupu, and there for his morning glass of rum goes the man who has travelled all night from a distant village. Nor are all the women here to buy or to sell. Those two who walk idly arm-in-arm are here to see and be seen, and they attain both objects very discreetly. That long-haired kilted native, with the strange melancholy face and the feminine air, is Maratai, the pet of the women, half woman and half man. He steps daintily and carries his market basket with the style of a lady shopping.

At last the crowd begins to disperse, bearing away its multitude of purchases: strings of fish, strings of cocoanuts, strings of breadfruit; bunches of bananas and *fei* slung on poles; meat and fruit in cocoanut-leaf baskets. We will not ourselves linger, for the market-place is dull without the people, and the policeman who has been collecting the vendor's tax will shortly start to yawn. Leaving the square we pass other Chinese stores and come to the harbour-side. On our right front, as we reach it, is the wharf. We turn to our left, to the quay where the schooners lie.

The warehouses are already open, the quay lively. Here is a schooner discharging pearl-shell, while a clerk and her supercargo check it as it is carried down her gangway bag by bag. That shell has come from a lagoon of the Paumotu atolls, and has all been got by swimming-divers, for the French Government forbids the use of the diving-dress, lest the deeps should be rifled and the breeding-beds of the pearl-oyster destroyed. Note the up-ended cannons which are planted along the quay as mooring-posts. A good instance of French economy. Here, further on, is a schooner loading. Her principal stores are aboard; her trade-room is full; and the wine and the rum are now being shipped. The man in the broad-brimmed hat, anxiously watching that cask being trundled aboard, is the captain of this vessel, which is bound for the Paumotus. For every cask and demijohn a permit has had to be obtained, the Paumotus being a 'dry' area; but a certain atoll will be dry only nominally when that cask has been delivered.

We will walk under the trees which shade the quay and shelter the busy and the idle, always found here in proximity, to the end of the line of schooners and the last warehouse; to Bougainville's monument and the naval steps. Over there on your left is the public pool, fed by a mountain stream, where the women wash clothes and all may bathe. Evening, not morning, is the popular bathing-hour, so the pool is vacant now. That double-storied building with galleries and green jalousies opening on the acacias, is the annexe of Lovaina's famous hotel. Opposite it the old French gunboat *Zelée*[1] rides at her anchor; that boatload of seamen is coming to drill on the quay. A little way further and we pass the escutcheon of the British Consulate; then the Protestant church and a succession of bungalows, which we leave to strike inland, and return by a parallel route, the Rue de Rivoli. The European who has just dashed from his doorway, to pick up that fallen mango, is not starving; he has a passion for the simple life, and lives upon fruit. He sits in his cottage and waits till he hears a mango fall in the street; then pounces on it, and devours it. He is realising his ideal of the South Sea existence.

The cathedral, the Casino Theatre, the Banque de l'Indo Chine: these bring us to the end of the Rue de Rivoli. Continuing, we come to the modest bungalow

[1] The *Zelée* was sunk during the bombardment by Admiral von Spee in 1914.

163

where the excellent Madame Lovaina has made herself the most celebrated of South Sea innkeepers; we cross a bridge over a clear brown river, and turning to our left by a Chinaman's store, enter a suburb. This is Patutoa, the sylvan home of the gay and the unconventional. The picturesque disorder of the scenery – the clumps of cocoa-nut and banana trees, the groves of breadfruit, the little wooden huts, the streams, the winding paths – suggest nothing so much as a stage set for the familiar South Sea drama. If we cross that field, from the other side of which comes the sound of singing voices, we shall discover a wine-party: the garlanded guests all seated in a ring about the demijohn, all singing, all swaying to their own music. But now the sun grows hot, so we will proceed and make a circuit back to town. Here, on your left, you have the old town ramparts, now overgrown with trees, yet still dividing the city, symbolically, from its Bohemia; and now we will cross this foot-bridge, which will take us by a straight road to the market-place. You have not seen all Papeete. You have not seen the schooner-building yard, nor the Faataua Avenue, with its giant trees, memorial of a lost civilisation: you have not seen the inland side of the town, where the well-born and the wealthy dwell at ease within walled and bosky gardens; but you have seen enough to give you an idea of the place.

I have said nothing of the inward charm of Tahiti, for that is entirely of the spirit and cannot be presented. It draws its strength from nothing one can name, and is as overpowering and elusive as the beauty of Helen. Of all places in the world Tahiti alone has given me that supreme happiness which touches anguish. But let no one go there believing that he will find what I found there. He may; but we find what is within us.

§ 2

I first became aware of a process of assimilation that was going on in me, when I realised that the steamer passengers, whether English or American, were foreigners. They were definitely not of my world. Their voices, faces, clothes and manners were disagreeable to me; they struck a jarring note. They spoiled the market crowd for me when they intruded on it; they were an offence wherever they appeared. Looking on their women, I saw them as pale ghosts beside the Tahiti women; and in my regard of the men I scarcely even made the distinction which the Polynesian makes, between the higher and the lower types. For the white man's colour he has no respect: to gain it, the individual must show his quality. Thus it comes about that the Polynesian has usually a just contempt for the foreign sailor and other inferior whites. I say 'just,' because the European's claim to superiority rests solely upon the achievements of a fractional percentage of higher minds. The civilised masses are lower – morally, mentally and physically – than is the savage. They are duller, more animal-like, and there is less kindness in them. Generally, they are less courageous. The inferior European may truly be called a degenerate savage, and the Polynesian recognises that.

This feeling of contempt is shared by the women. The worst thing one native woman can say of another is that she associates with foreign sailors. In Tahiti that is indeed the limit of feminine degradation. This being so, it can scarcely be wondered at that Papeete should be rated by master mariners as, for disease, one of the worst ports in the world. Incredible scenes of debauchery take place on shore and on shipboard, but the women who take part in these are few, and constitute, rather than belong to, the lowest class. I doubt if more than a dozen could ever be found at one time in Papeete. Light girls, on the other hand, are legion, but it would be wrong to call these prostitutes. 'Philanderers' fits them better. They live for lovers, but not all of them by means of lovers. Very many of them are working girls. About a quarter are of Tahitian birth; the rest come from all parts of the Eastern Pacific.

Men also come to Papeete in large numbers, and so strong are the brown population's foreign constituents, that the Rarotongans, the Paumotuans and other races occupy separate quarters. Next to these indigenous peoples the most numerous element is the Chinese, who have the whole of the small shopkeeping trade in their hands, and are beginning to compete with the big traders. Following them closely come the Europeans – French, English, Germans – and Americans, who fill the official positions, run the warehouses and officer the schooners; and a medley of Japanese, Indians, negroes and Spanish-Americans make up the tail of the census.

The last-named – the Hispanioles and their half-caste

progeny – are responsible for most of the crimes of passion, which, however, are rare. Other crimes of violence are even rarer, and suicide, among the natives, is almost unknown. When it occurs, it is the result of a sudden ungovernable impulse. The Polynesian has not the temperament for suicide; his is the robust spirit of Shakespearian comedy, and his gaiety is proof against most common ills. He looks for a like gaiety in the foreigner, and abhors the sour and the long face. In his cups he is jovial and seldom quarrelsome. Bad-tempered children and quarrelsome adults are in Tahiti equally exceptional.

With regard to the oft-repeated charge of immodesty, it may be said that the Tahitian's modesty is not ours. On the other hand, his sense of it is strong enough to make him charge us with immodesty. A woman of Tahiti once said to me: 'White men have no shame' – and in the account of the first missionary voyage[1] it is recorded that the Otaheitans say: 'Englishmen are ashamed of nothing.' This missionary writer states also that 'they have in many instances more refined ideas of decency than ourselves.'

While writing of Tahiti I cannot let the opportunity pass of saying a word in praise of the Chinaman, whose commercial morality is so high that a native will trust him rather than he will trust an English trader. I never knew or heard of a case in which a Chinaman broke his word. Add to his integrity his shrewdness, his industry and his good-nature, and it is no wonder that the trade of the

[1] *A Missionary Voyage to the Southern Pacific.*

French Pacific is falling into his hands. Once he has it, he will never let it go, for, established, no one can compete with him.

§ 3

When I had made that discovery I have mentioned, of the steamer passengers being foreigners to me, I determined that I must make Tahiti my home; that this was destined. I had not a shadow of regret that this was to be so; but I hoped to extend my knowledge of the South Seas, and to have the experience of trading. I had made an essay in South Sea matrimony, but the experiment, through unwise selection on my part, had not been successful. I meant now to make another trial of it, as a prelude to my settlement here; but before I could carry out this purpose, an ill thing befell me.

I had been more than two years at Papehui, and had managed the plantation for some months while Tauraa was in America, which had given me increased status and increased pay, and a continuance of my responsibilities on his return. This was why I had not sought a change of employment, though I might ere this have launched myself into trading.

Now for an account of what befell me.

I woke one morning, lit a cigarette, as my habit was, and throwing off the sheet sat up in bed. I then noticed, at first with doubt but soon with certainty, that my feet were not quite alike. My right foot was fleshier than my left: there was a slight puffiness behind the ankle and in front of the instep. There was no mark of a bite or a sting to be found; nor did I feel any pain or stiffness in the foot. Nevertheless, I concluded that some insect had bitten me during the night.

The foot was still puffy the next morning, and I examined it more closely. I then found some tiny red marks, barely discernible, like the minute veins in marble. 'Puffy' hardly describes the condition of the flesh: it was as though an extra layer of perfectly healthy fat had grown over the parts affected.

Rheumatism, or what I took to be rheumatism, had recently laid me up for two or three days, but that had attacked me in the other leg. I guessed, however, now that there was some connection between it and the present peculiar symptoms. Being not at all alarmed, I mentioned the matter to nobody; and after a week, when the foot showed no alteration, I grew quite used to the sight of it.

A fortnight passed, and I then had a sharp attack of fever. It was like my old friend, the fever and ague, except that burning pains shot through my foot and up the calf to the knee. Quinine drove out the fever and quelled the shiverings; I slept, and woke in the morning weak and tired, but not otherwise ill. There was a feeling of discomfort, though, in the foot, and on turning the piled bed-clothes from it, I saw a great change. It was red and puffed from toe to heel, and the swelling extended above the ankle. There was a soreness, also, and stiffness in the joints when I moved them, and the sole of the foot was tender.

I became afraid. I rose and dressed, and took the stage to Papeete, to see a doctor. He spoke the word I feared – Elephantiasis – and said I had got the disease through going barefoot: it was contracted in several ways, but that was the commonest.

He was consolatory. It might be years, he said, before my leg became an obvious deformity. Progress was sometimes rapid, but more often it was slow. Intemperance and neglect were the most frequent causes of rapid progress; he knew a man who had had the disease for two years, without his friends being aware of it. There was another point which I was to bear in mind – a most important point: a change of climate would usually work a complete cure in the early stages, and would check the disease at any stage. He told me further that I need not be distressed about the present state of my foot. In a couple of days the inflammation would be gone, and my foot would be only a little more fleshy than it had been. The inflammation would return with each attack, and the attacks – that is, the fever and the pains – would decrease in intensity. The most painful period of the malady was at its commencement.

He was a most cheerful physician.

His diagnosis was verified: I will not bore the reader with details of the advance of the disease. I suffered little inconvenience from it except during the attacks; but I could not blink the fact that my foot was growing; and the other had become affected. I was able to wear my boots, but I foresaw the day when my legs would fill my trousers; when I should be like poor Robson. I abandoned my matrimonial plans, and was driven reluctantly to consider the advisability of leaving the island.

Once faced, I found the logic of the case hard to resist. I had little money in hand, but I could save some, and I had almost decided to go, when I received an unexpected draft from England, which put hesitation from me.

My last month in Tahiti I spent in town, doing my best to banish melancholy. I felt that I was leaving all I cared for on earth, to resume a wandering life which had now no attraction for me. The sight of the quayside schooners saddened me with the thought that I had never sailed in one of them, never seen the wild Paumotus nor the famed Marquesas. But I resolutely rejected the idea that I was not to return. If what everyone told me was true about the effect of a change of climate, there was no reason why I should not hope for a speedy return.

I had a cabin in Patutoa, and I passed the last night on its verandah, sitting in a wicker chair. A girl was with me, and she sat on my lap and fell asleep there, her head against my shoulder; and so we sat till morning, sleeping and waking, smoking cigarettes and talking. She was tired of the common ways of love, she told me; and so, just then, was I.

Tahiti from the sea is, I think, the most beautiful object visible to the eye of man. Its beauty is fantastic; it belongs to fairy-land: an earthly beauty purified of earth's grossness. It passed from my sight about five o'clock of the following afternoon, and I was not to see it again for nearly four years.

After an uneventful passage I arrived in New Zealand in December of the year 1912.

CHAPTER XII

★

§ 1

WELLINGTON, where I landed, roused aversion in me. It was so pallid, bare and chill; so cheerless. Bleak, in a word, as I had noticed before, but never so bleak as I saw it now. Its people too had a bleak look. They hurried about the streets, engrossed in affairs, wearing stony expressions and hideous clothes. Their rapt haste in particular annoyed me. Why the devil were they all in such a hurry? I thought them a little demented, and reflected that, if they were, the whole of the European world was equally demented. That idea has never deserted me.

However, one grows used to most things, and one may grow used to living in a demented world. At the end of two days I did not like Wellington any better, but its strangeness was less glaring; and I had found that it was not mad in all its units; there were perfectly sane individuals. A pretty chambermaid who brought my tea in the morning convinced me fully of this fact.

But I could not afford to dally with pretty chambermaids: my money was running out: and I saw no means of acquiring more in Wellington. I therefore took a boat for the South Island, knowing that the rabbit-poisoning season would be starting at St. Helens. I had hardly arrived in Christchurch when I had one of my attacks of fever. It was a severe one and laid me out for a day. My legs, I ought to mention, were as serviceable as ever, between the attacks, and upon the day following this one I was able to visit the employment agent.

Fortune favoured me. St. Helens wanted men, and I left for Hanmer that evening. Charlie, the Dutch ganger, greeted me warmly, and I was very glad to meet him again.

In due course we went up to the hills. I had told Charlie of my trouble, and that, having had one bout in New Zealand, I might expect another, so he was not surprised when I had to fall out one morning and make my way back to camp. I had less than two miles to go, but it was a tough march. At last I reached the tents, and dropped, completely done, upon my blankets, to the great concern of the cook, whom my ague led to think that I was about to expire. It was certainly very violent on this occasion, and I do not remember to have had a worse attack. It proved to be the last. It was not I but the malady which was making the death struggle. In the afternoon I was able to swallow some soup. The next morning I was too exhausted to go out, but was fit for duty the day after.

From that day my legs began to lessen. As I need not mention them again, I may say here that before six months were past they had come to their normal dimensions. My feet alone showed a disposition to swell sometimes, after long standing or walking; but before very long this passed away also.

A nephew of Swinburne was this year a member of our gang. He was another old Cape Mounted Rifleman whose acquaintance I had made at Kokstad (where I had first met Goddard, you may remember). He had been well known there as a gentleman jockey, and was more widely known in New Zealand as a rider and trainer of horses. His health had not been good lately, and he had come here, as so many others did, for pedestrian exercise and the tonic of the mountain air. He spoke of his uncle respectfully but without enthusiasm. I don't know why, but I gathered that the subject of Uncle Algernon was slightly embarrassing. The Swinburnes were not accustomed to breeding poets; they went in more for admirals. A poet was a marked divergence from type. One had to acknowledge his fame, since all the world acknowledged it; but in one's heart one could have wished that he had acquired it otherwise.

This was simply the impression I gathered, and I may be far wrong.

The first snow was long in coming, but at length we looked out one morning on a white world. We made such preparations as we could for an early departure, as the packman was expected to arrive as soon as the weather cleared. We did not anticipate a long wait, as the first fall of the autumn is seldom heavy. But a couple of days passed, and the snow still fell, and the sky, instead of lightening, was becoming murkier. The drifts were in places six feet deep.

It appeared as if this fall was not the usual precursor to the fall which yearly closed the passes, but the heavy fall itself. The same thought must have struck the station manager, for the horses struggled up our gully on the third day, and the orders were that we were to come in immediately. That was easier said than done, but, apart from orders, there was no option but to start. To stay longer would have been to endanger our lives.

The tents and baggage were packed, and the train set out. We were eighteen miles from the out-station. The packman took the route by which he had come, but owing to its obstacles, of rivers, which were now swollen with snow, he thought this route impracticable for us. We, therefore, under the guidance of Charlie, cut out a track for ourselves. We had one river-crossing to make, and that we made straightway. The cold of the water was so intense that I had no sensation in my feet for nearly an hour afterwards, though we walked at as rapid a pace as the deep snow would permit. Its depth averaged eighteen inches, and the leader, of course, had the worst of it. When Charlie tired I replaced him, and afterwards the most capable among us took turns at breaking the road. Even for those who followed, it was very laborious walking. One plunged into drifts waist-deep, from which the weaker members of the party had now and then to be extricated. By noon we saw that we should have our work cut out to reach the station by nightfall. The snow had stopped, and the sun came out for some hours, but about four o'clock the sky darkened, and snow fell more heavily than ever. Our way was through the valley of a river, and the scene was wild and threatening in the extreme as day closed in upon us. To walk demanded now an effort of will for each step that was taken. We had long ago lost sight of the packman, but had heard the crack of his whip for a few minutes from somewhere behind the snow curtain.

Two men who were more knocked up than the rest of us were our chief danger. We had to accommodate our pace to theirs, and were constantly in fear of their collapsing. Were this to happen, two of us would have to stay with them, and try to bring them on; and those left behind might easily perish. To lie down in a snow-storm is dangerous, when the body is exhausted; to sleep in it, usually fatal, if rescue is not speedy. All of us, I believe, had the strongest desire to lie down, if only for five minutes, but we well knew the danger of doing so, and somehow we all kept going.

The night, when it came, was almost pitch-dark, but the river roared on our left, and this was our guide. It was now, however, impossible to pick our way, and we could only flounder on, through drifts and over rocky ridges. To my dismay, I saw that Charlie himself was at last cracking up. He had been a magnificent leader and had borne the brunt of the work. I struck a match and looked at my watch: it was eight o'clock. Someone called to the last of our stragglers, and there was a faint answer. We in the lead had halted.

I thought I detected a sound, far off and muffled. It was so disguised by the snow that its character was not at first recognizable. Someone else heard it, and we listened.

'Dogs!' gasped Charlie.

177

We raised our united voices in a call, and picked up an answer.

The knowledge that a search party was out for us acted like brandy, and failing legs struck out again. We were now on a broad flat, which the dogs were methodically coursing, and half an hour after we had heard them we made contact with the shepherds. Fortunately they had brought horses, or our troubles would not even now have been over, for we were some distance from the out-station. A flask of whisky passed from mouth to mouth, and we then mounted, or were hoisted, to the horses. The ratio was one horse for two men, and I double-banked with Charlie. Being behind, I was the first to dismount at the end of our journey. I slipped down gaily enough, but as soon as my feet touched the ground my legs crumpled under me, and I lay on my back in the snow. At this diverting performance the pair of us roared with laughter. It seemed the richest of jokes. Charlie got down more cautiously, and helped me up.

We ate an enormous supper – and how very bright that room looked after the darkness! how warm was the fire of logs on the big hearth! Food and warmth and tobacco revived us amazingly. I slept like a stone that night and awoke almost fresh – fresh enough, at any rate, to make no bones of a tramp of fourteen miles, which brought us to the homestead. But we had a good road, the sun was shining again, and the snow-fall had not been heavy on the flanks of the mountains.

In Hanmer I said good-bye to Charlie. He, with most

of the others, went to Christchurch: I stayed and worked for some months for the Forestry Department, which was making extensive plantations on Hanmer Plains. The severity of the weather drove me also to Christchurch in mid-winter, and from there I went north, for a milder climate. Near Hastings I found work on a farm, where I pulled mangel-wurzels, cleared dikes and occasionally drove a cart, until summer-time brought hay-making. This farm was like a bit of England. The manager was a Northumbrian, the head carter a Yorkshireman, and the cart-horses answered to such names as Kate and Dick and Blossom. The stock names of horses and cows seem to be preserved throughout the English-speaking world. You would hardly find a farm in Australasia where there is not a cow named Strawberry. That may not be very remarkable, but it sharply reminds one of what one is apt to forget – the continuity of British tradition.

The hay-making was thoroughly to my taste. I worked on the stack, and took almost as much pride in it as the stacker, an ancient English rustic. After the harvest came the sheep-dipping, and just before Easter I left, having stayed here much longer than I had thought to stay. But I found something soothing in the work, and something satisfying in the change of occupation which each month brought with it.

I could not yet safely return to Tahiti, and decided, in default, to revisit Sydney, a town of pleasant memories.

I arrived there early in April. Easter is Sydney's festive season, and is usually blessed with ideal weather, as it was upon this occasion. I therefore improved the shining hour till my pockets were nearly empty.

Then for the bush. I took the train to the port of New-castle, and from there struck out for the west. I came at last to a somewhat remote township of the name of Coolah, and here heard of a station which wanted axe-men. Thither I travelled by a long and lonely road amidst tall bush. The bush roads of Australia are so much alike that you may travel for hundreds of miles in some parts and see no change in the character of the scenery. You might even imagine sometimes that you were in the very place you left a week ago. The bush scenery – the blue and white and red gums, the gray-green delicate foliage, the shadows in the silky dust of the road – has its unquestionable beauty, but the repetition of it becomes tiresome. One may travel far in the temperate zones of the earth and find nothing of charm so enduring, of beauty so diverse, as the English countryside.

I interviewed the manager of the station and was engaged and sent to a camp.

§ 2

On a certain fine, crisp day in the early part of August, we were visited, while at work, by the station manager. He sat on his horse and told us that he had important news. He then began to read from a newspaper an announcement of Great Britain's declaration of war upon Germany.

We leaned on our axes and listened. We had heard of

the murder in Serajevo and of trouble which had arisen from it, but this was the first news we had had of war. We were all appropriately thrilled. I imagined a sort of Franco-Prussian war, on a very much bigger scale, but not differing from it in kind.

The manager, a Little Australian of the old school, remarked that while the news would interest all of us, it had a special importance for Englishmen. We (the Englishmen) would probably be expected to go and fight.

He rode off and we resumed our work. There was very little discussion. Men were thinking.

Newspapers, hitherto rare, began now to reach the camp daily, being sent out to us by the manager. I became very restless, and at length informed the ganger that I was going away.

There was dissatisfaction in the camp at this time, and the news that I was going had no sooner circulated, than the men, one by one, followed my example.

The job was nearly finished, and the manager was angry with the lot of us, but furious with me, for having, as he believed, seduced his men. Had his tone been more moderate we might have retracted: as it was, we rolled our swags and went; and I suppose, if that manager ever recalls me, he still thinks of me as an agitator.

I rode into Coolah on a spare horse that one of our men had with him; stayed the night at an inn, and caught a coach in the morning for the nearest railway point. I was in Sydney by night.

After breakfast, while I was walking up George Street,

considering whether I should go to the barracks at once or wait a day or two, I saw in the crowd a face I seemed to know. It belonged to a burly man about my own age, rather dark, with a little dark moustache and well-bred features. He was dressed like a working-man from the bush, but his face told that he was not an ordinary working-man. He seemed to recognise me, and we stopped and regarded each other.

'I can't place you,' I said. 'Where have we met?'

He was as hazy as I was about this. 'South Africa?' he suggested. 'New Guinea? Tahiti? – '

Remembrance flashed upon us simultaneously. We had met twice in Tahiti, once at the house of an acquaintance, once in the market-place. His name, I remembered, was Meredith, and he had been spending a long holiday there.

We had a drink, and talked of Tahiti and the war. He too had thought of enlisting, but was doubtful if it would not be better to enlist in England. The Australian troops, he feared, might never see the front.

We spent the day together, and evolved a plan. There was a chance, we thought, that the war might be a short one, and we did not wish to enlist, either here or in England, and find, when ready for the field, that we were not wanted. By waiting six weeks or a couple of months, we could form a better opinion of the probable length of the war, and we might also be better able to decide if it was worth while to go to England. If it seemed so, we should need all the money we had, and in consequence could not afford to remain in Sydney. In the bush we might earn money instead of spending it, so thither we resolved to go.

Our travels, by boot, started from Goulburn, and after working for a fortnight on a new railway line, we tramped at a leisurely pace and without any special object except to kill time, through an area of small country towns and farms.

Our fortnight's work had given us pocket-money, so we lived more luxuriously than swagmen usually live, and fried our eggs and bacon regularly for breakfast. One evening we managed to lose our way and found ourselves in a woodless and waterless country where there was no prospect of a good camp. We arrived at length at a farm, and determined, if possible, to camp there.

We said we were looking for work, and we were rather taken aback when work was offered to us. The farmer, an elderly man, had a paddock to be grubbed, and he thought we were just the men to do it. He was letting the job on contract, at so much an acre. We replied that we would consider it in the morning, if he would allow us to stay the night.

It so happened that we were nearly out of food supplies, having intended to reprovision ourselves at a store which we had missed by taking the wrong road. Half a loaf of bread, I think, was all we had; but it was fortunate for us that we had that, for we were given a very poor supper. After a breakfast that was little better, we went out with our host to look at the job.

Neither it nor the terms he offered were very attractive.

However, we thought we might put it through in a week, and after a short private consultation we told him that we would undertake it. We added that we must have rations at once, and these he promised to send.

We then pitched our tent, and tools having arrived, we set to work.

We did not say very much for the first hour. The roots, which went deeper than we had supposed, demanded all our attention. Then Meredith straightened his back and addressed me:

'We sha'n't see the end of this in three weeks, and it'll pay us at the rate of about half-a-crown a day, minus our rations.'

I had already reached a like opinion, and I hastened to express my agreement with him.

'But we've got no tucker,' I observed, 'and we're twenty miles from anywhere. My inside is nothing but a cavity now.'

At that moment a horse and cart and man appeared on the crest of a hill behind which was the farm.

'There's our tucker, at any rate,' said Meredith. 'The best thing we can do is to fill our bags and hop it. That whiskered old thief deserves to be done.'

He did; but we let him down lightly. The cart delivered our rations and retreated, and we slogged away at the roots till it was out of sight. We calculated that we had done four shillings' worth of work (by our, not the farmer's, reckoning), and we helped ourselves to about four shillings' worth of tucker; struck our tent, rolled our swags, and legged it. We made a detour to avoid the farm, and came out on the road which we had last night been following. Further on we came to a cross-road with a sign-post. There was wood here; we were carrying water, and we halted and boiled the billy.

Taking the cross-road, we reached a small township at sunset, and after supper explored it. There was not much to see, and having seen it, we entered a hotel. There were several people in the bar, and among them a pugilistic-looking person who showed a desire to be offensive. Very foolishly, he suggested that Meredith could not fight. In less than a brace of shakes he was being disillusioned. His friends, seeing that he was getting the worst of it, attempted to stop the duel, but a clout apiece sent them to a safer distance, and Meredith then requested me to clear the bar. This I was able to do without coming to blows, whereupon I mounted guard on the one doorway. The landlord, at the commencement of the fray, had rushed from the bar, and the reason of this move became apparent while I was standing in the posture of Horatius.

I looked round. Meredith's opponent was very groggy.

'Finish him off as quickly as you can,' I said. 'Here's a policeman coming.'

I did not wish to retire before the work was done, but neither did I wish for a brush with the law. The policeman, a trooper, was obliging enough not to hurry matters. As he came nearer I saw that he was elderly and not very robust. He stopped to ask some questions of the bystanders, and I heard, to my relief, the fall of a heavy body. Leaving

his man on the floor, Meredith joined me, and we walked
– *mirabile dictu!* – past the trooper without his attempting
to stay us. I imagine that the landlord had given him a
horrific account of Meredith, and he was only too glad
to see the last of two evident desperadoes. He was, we
heard later, the sole policeman here, and near the end of
his service.

To escape any unpleasantness, we broke camp at an
early hour in the morning. Whether it was that this little
scrimmage had excited us, or we were reminded that our
energies might be better employed than in bar-room
scuffles, I cannot now recall, but this day we decided to
enlist without further postponement.

We took train to Sydney and presented ourselves next
morning at Victoria Barracks. Almost the first person I
met here was a sergeant who had been a friend of mine at
Thursday Island.

'I thought I knew your hard old dial!' was his greeting,
which, if not very polite, was cordially meant.

We were taken to the sergeants' mess, and when he had
regaled us, we joined the queue which was waiting to pass
the colonel.

It is quaint now to think of the eagerness of the candi-
dates, and of the extreme care with which they were
chosen. None but men with some military training had a
chance of passing the colonel, and many of these, for one
reason or another, were rejected; and the medical examination was equally strict. Meredith and I were successful
and were sent with a party of recruits to Rosehill, a race-

course that was being utilised as a training-camp. There were insufficient tents and we slept on the grand-stand. The 4th Brigade was forming at Rosehill, and had we stayed with it we might have got early promotion; but at our first morning parade there was a call for volunteers to go to the 1st Division. The 1st Division, we knew, was soon to embark; we exchanged glances, stepped to the front, and were accepted.

Thus it happened that we joined the 1st Brigade not many days before it sailed, when its non-commissioned ranks had permanent occupants. On our way to the camp, Meredith and I were accidentally separated, and before we fully realised what had occurred, he was being marched off to the 1st and I to the 4th Battalion. We tried afterwards for a transfer, but neither of our company commanders was willing to part with us, and we embarked in different ships, he in the *Afric,* I a day later in the *Euripides.*

CHAPTER XIII

★

§ 1

THE voyage had one interesting moment, when we came in touch with the *Emden*. For three nights before that we had slept at boat-stations. The *Euripides*, in which were the 3rd and 4th Battalions and about five hundred men of the Army Medical Corps and other details, led the starboard of the three lines of transports, and leading us was a Japanese cruiser. We were aware that something was happening when one morning, while at drill on the boat-deck, we saw the Japanese cruiser suddenly turn in and steam rapidly to port. She came back and we were then informed that the *Emden* had been sighted and the *Sydney* had gone after her. Before noon came the news that the *Emden* was a wreck on Cocos Island and the *Sydney* not much damaged. Beer was issued every day at noon, and on this day we were allowed two pints instead of one, a privilege of which few did not avail themselves. The Fourth in particular was a thirsty battalion.

Our passage through the Canal was a slow but interesting progress. Indian troops in wired encampments lined its banks, and we passed several transports crowded with French troops. Up till now our destination was unknown to us: many thought that we were going to England: but before we were out of the Canal we learned that it was Alexandria. We had not set foot on land since leaving Sydney; and after six weeks in a crowded ship we were glad to go ashore anywhere. We saw

188

nothing of Alexandria but its harbour-side, as we stepped from the wharf to the train.

From Cairo railway station, where we arrived late, my company marched to the Kasr-el-Nil Barracks, and, without undressing, we passed the night on a verandah. In the morning we joined the rest of the battalion, which had been billeted elsewhere, and took the road for Mena and the Pyramids. We were all in the highest spirits, not only at being ashore, but to be in a land of such intriguing strangeness, and under a sky as blue as that of Australia. We viewed the Pyramids with awe when first we sighted them, and the thoughts of many must have been that, but for the war, we should probably never have looked upon these wonders. Our satisfaction grew when we found that we were to camp almost at the foot of them.

Our tents not having arrived, we bivouacked the first night, and by a remarkable fatality were drenched with rain. I was told that rain was so rare in Egypt that this was the first which had fallen for a couple of years. I don't know if this was true, but I do know that it never rained again during our four months' stay here. The tents arrived in the course of the day, and we pitched camp.

§ 2

I came to love the desert. It was our drill ground, and most of our training was done in it. The monotony of its colouring never wearied me, for this was balanced by the multiplicity of its features. Hill and valley and bluff, mountains and plains, every familiar detail of a fertile country was there – all but the grass, the brooks, the hedges and the trees. One could please oneself by clothing it with verdure, by populating it with villages. A fertile land leaves nothing to the imagination; but it is to the imagination that the desert makes its strongest appeal. Sometimes I saw its plains rippled by the wind, in the likeness of a wind-rippled inland sea.

A peculiarity of its atmosphere which we noticed early was its magnification of objects not a part of it. Men at a few hundred yards' distance had the seeming stature of giants; and the lightness of its colour made our khaki uniforms appear dark brown. A camel patrol proceeding in single file along the desert road looked monstrous. My eyes never got used to this illusion of size.

Wherever we went we were followed by blue-robed fellaheen with oranges and hard-boiled eggs to sell. Some of them spent whole days on the flanks of our column, like Bedouins waiting a chance to raid a merchants' train. Their chance came when we halted and sat down; not till then were they allowed to approach us. We conceived the idea that oranges and eggs were the sole products of Egypt, and that the sand cooked the eggs as the hens laid them. We seldom met an egg that was not hard-boiled.

Our training was pretty severe, but it was so modulated that it did not over-tax us. Even so, it searched out the weak spots and eliminated many hundreds (from the Division, of course) who had stood the lighter Australian training. A man who went through what we went through in the desert was fit to go anywhere and do any-thing, and it was a fortunate thing that we were so rigor-ously tested. I should say that it was mainly the Aus-tralians' desert work which enabled them to secure the heights of Gallipoli. Hardest of all was our brigade train-ing; in this we became finally inured to hunger, fatigue and thirst. The crown of it was a forty-eight hours' operation during which we marched and manoeuvred almost ceaselessly.

I had been given the distinguished job of Battle Orderly, a high-sounding title which the war soon shortened into 'runner.' There was one for each company and one for the battalion, and my field duty was to carry verbal mes-sages from the colonel to my company commander. In practice it amounted to rather more, for it was found that I could memorize a message more accurately than the others, so that any long or intricate message was usually entrusted to me. These errands had to be executed at the double, and my legs had thus plenty of exercise. But I rather liked the job, as it gave me an interesting insight into operations, and freed me from the tedium of company work. Also, I found a pleasure in attending the colonel. He was a man who could be very courteous and agreeable to a private, without a suggestion of condescension or the least peril to his dignity. That a colonel should be cour-teous and agreeable to a private may seem odd, but Colonel Onslow Thompson was an Australian sheep-owner and had no traditions of aloofness.

Our bands were a great solace at Mena. It was most

pleasant, in camp, to hear the brave music draw nearer and nearer from the desert as a band played its battalion up to the parade-ground. All the tunes they played have lingered in my memory, so that if I recall one of them now, I have a vision of the battalion which used to march to it — winding in, a long dark snake upon the sand, to that great array of tents before the Pyramids. Those remembered tunes are among the most moving and vivid of all my memories. They do not merely recall, they recreate.

Our own band was a failure. Because many of our officers were of Scottish extraction we had the pipes, but on the march these were scarcely audible beyond the leading company. There was nothing the matter with the pipers except that there was not enough of them. We envied the battalions which had brass bands, and we commended the sense of the Fifth, which also claimed to be Scottish, but had brass and pipes.

Since coming to Mena, I had, as was natural, seen Meredith often, but our being in different battalions had parted us in a way which only a soldier will understand. The corps spirit made us cleave to our respective families, for the corps is the soldier's family, and its bond is as strong as any family bond. Brothers in arms, while they are such, are even more to one another than blood brothers, and outside the unit all are aliens; so that Meredith and I met as divided friends. Our feelings for each other had not altered, but our circumstances having totally changed, had changed our relations. We recognized that this was inevitable, and that it was a temporary sundering.

We planned a return to Tahiti – after the war. We talked very lovingly of the island; but not longingly; at least, not with open longing. We promised ourselves six months of complete idleness in that place where, we agreed, one could idle more pleasantly than in any place we knew. How lazily we would lounge on cool verandahs; how blissfully we would sup our morning coffee and watch the market crowd, and drink white wine at Pepe's!

We talked in this way, but we did not blind ourselves to the likelihood that there might be no 'after the war' for us.

§ 3

Cairo I visited as often as I had the opportunity, but my difficulty was to see enough of the place in the half-day leaves allowed us. This difficulty was felt by many, and we overcame it by the obvious and only possible means. At Christmas time the absentees in my battalion numbered over three hundred, and this led the colonel to threaten us with a special button, to make us readily distinguishable to our pickets. The button never materialized, because shortly after this we were given shoulder colours, a method of distinguishing unit from unit which caused no heartburnings.

For me, though the European quarter soon staled, the native town never lost its attraction. Few haunts of humanity have so interested me as those teeming, fetid, garish, serpentine streets where the humble Cairene dwells with the surprising contentment noticeable in the slum-dweller everywhere. It is a curious fact that one sees more smiling faces in a slum than in a prosperous suburb. One may imagine either that slum life is actually pleasant or that its hardships breed a spirit proportionate to it.

In scenes of the utmost squalor one would come upon such an incongruous sight as a school and hear the children chanting their lessons as in a school in England. I remember one well: it was in an upper room; the scholars sat on forms, and the schoolmaster, catching sight of the Australian soldier, came to the window to greet him. That Egyptian dominie's face was of the true dominie type, austere yet mild; and he smiled gravely at me as I passed by. Somehow he brought my surroundings into better focus. I was able to perceive a unity in them, in place of a bizarre disorder. East and West had met.

This was the quarter of the very poor. A quarter much frequented by the troops was a labyrinth of alleys in the neighbourhood of the Esbekiya Gardens. Here there were cafés, dance-halls and other attractions, and here the Egyptian showed himself at his beastliest. The truth of Darwin's biological deductions could be clearly proved, if any proof were needed, by the likenesses of men to various animals. Who can look at a pig, especially a Berkshire, without observing how extraordinarily human he is? And the likeness (in his manners) of a certain type of Egyptian to an ape makes the relationship unquestionable. Flecker noticed it and referred to it in *Hassan*. But no ape could conceive the obscenities which were exhibited in the little back rooms of the quarter to which I am now referring. They shocked me, and I have seen a good deal. They were the dreams of a sexual maniac in an asylum, and obscenity is really no name for them.

Some of the cafés about here were little, quiet places, kept by an Abdul or Achmet, where baggy-trousered graybeards smoked the narghile, and one could drink Turkish coffee or Greek wine. Others partook more of the nature of beer-halls, and had waitresses who danced with customers when required. Those were principally patronized by the soldiery, of whom there were many varieties in Cairo at this time. Besides our own men there were the New Zealanders (with whom they fought), English Territorials, Indians, Fellaheen and Soudanese. In the narrow ways of the popular amusement quarter uniforms were far more conspicuous than the native robe. There was one large café chantant, a decently-conducted place, where none but soldiers were to be seen. Here Sikh cavalrymen in steel-quoited turbans hobnobbed with slouch-hatted Colonials, and bestowed polite attention upon the cancan.

The winter nights were cold, and roast-chestnut men did a good trade in the Esbekiya Square. Their presence gave one at first a sense of the incongruous; but Asia Minor is of course the home of the sweet chestnut. A pocketful of hot roast chestnuts somewhat mitigated the rigours of the ride home, when one had, as often as not, to cling to the foot-board of a tram rushing to Mena in a sharp head wind. Then blankets and a sound sleep till réveillé.

In speaking of Cairo I have said not a word of the mosques, Saladin's citadel, the bazaars, the museum, the zoo, or any of the prescribed sights. I have not even mentioned the water-sellers, the jugglers or the wild dervishes. Did I, therefore, miss these interesting spectacles, or deliberately close my eyes to them? Well, no; but there are guide-books.

But I should not pass the ladies by without a word. Their beauty I was prepared for; the freedom of their glances was a surprise to me, who had expected an almost nun-like bearing in these veiled women. But that scrap of white muslin could hardly be called a veil: instead of hiding, it enhanced their beauty. They were, to my eye, far more lovely than the women of Southern Europe, and in many cases fairer-skinned.

The black-veiled women of the lower class were much less attractive, being swarthy and plain-featured. Some were chaste, some were not, and some who were really prostitutes wore the veil. But, as a rule, the prostitutes went unveiled. The number of native prostitutes, however, was small compared with the vast army of foreign women from every country in Europe, most of whom should have been smothered or kept in lock hospitals until the war was over. The majority had been expelled by the police from their own countries, and the damage they did to our troops is too well-known to need telling.

CHAPTER XIV

★

§ 1

IT was a heterogeneous force which was camped on the
field of Napoleon's battle with the Mamelukes. About
60 per cent were Australians; English, Scotch and Irish
composed about 30 per cent, and the remainder was
made up chiefly of Frenchmen, Belgians, Russians,
Italians and Maltese. But it was not merely the different
nationalities which made the force so mixed; its diversity
showed more in the different kinds of men. There were
old soldiers, adventurers, sincere patriots, men who had
enlisted to escape their wives or their creditors, and others
to whom five shillings a day and rations were the principal or sole attraction. There were many who dreamed
of glory and some who hoped for death; and there were
not a few professional gamblers who expected to make a
pile. But the patriots were unquestionably in the majority,
and, wasters though there were, I doubt if any finer body
of fighting-men was ever gathered together. I need not
add that it was recruited from all classes. Of my tent-
mates, one, the lance-corporal, was an Australian farmer's
son; another was a young Anglo-Indian; a third was an
ex-naval man; a fourth was a butcher; a fifth was a bank
clerk; two were railwaymen; two were labourers; one
was a drover; one was a linendraper. The Anglo-Indian
was perhaps the most remarkable of them; his zeal was
almost fanatical. He was abstaining from tobacco, alcohol
and all indulgences for the period of the war. He slept

invariably with his boots on, in order to inure himself to field conditions. Two days' fighting was all he was destined to see.

The two railwaymen, bush lads, talked of nothing but home and future plans. One was going to buy a motor-cycle; the other had a girl and was to be married. Both were very good shots and exemplary soldiers. These two were killed in the first week. The clerk, a lively youth, rather fond of beer, went shortly after them; the naval man, a gay and gallant spirit, with whom I was particularly intimate, lived three months; and one of the two labourers was the last to go. Four, including the lance-corporal, left the Peninsula with wounds and were invalided to Australia; another went temporarily insane, and one alone of the twelve of us reached France, where tuberculosis claimed him. That, in brief, was the family record.

The South African mounted police forces were well represented in the Division; in my company were two of my old Rhodesian comrades. One was a sergeant-major, and had the bad luck to be shot through the head while shaving, on the day of his promotion to lieutenant. His mirror had betrayed him. I met but one old Royal Australian gunner, but I know that there were many with us.

§ 2

During January, February and March many rumours circulated as to where we were to be sent when we were fit for war. With the knowledge that the Fleet was to attack the Dardanelles, the most prevalent of these rumours came to be that we were to be employed to garrison Constantinople. I spoke to Meredith about this, and his reply was that he thought it probable, as garrison duty was about all we were fit for. Loyal as he was to his battalion, he placed little reliance on Australian valour. Distrust of the Australian's fighting qualities was an obsession of his. I am glad now to think that I did not share it.

But what was even more odd was that the men themselves distrusted their military abilities. They referred to themselves constantly as the Rag-time Army, the Five-Bob-a-Day Tourists, and the Keystone Comedy Company. It was evident to me that these were no mere jests intended to hide self-confidence, but an earnest and bitter criticism of themselves. They were just those 'half-baked' troops, they said, that Kitchener had expressly stated he didn't want, and the rumours of garrison duty at Constantinople were accepted with resignation. India was mentioned, and Palestine, but always it was taken for granted that we should not be given an important part to play. All ranks held this opinion. In a first-rate war, how could second-rate troops hope for an important rôle?

The Australian is often regarded as a conceited braggart, but never did he show his true self better than in his modesty while he lay at Mena awaiting the call.

A rumour did at length begin to gain ground that before we reached Constantinople we might see a little fighting. It was now said that we were to be landed on Turkish territory after the Fleet had prepared a way for us, and that we might have the Greeks as partners. It became tolerably certain that we were going to do something soon when General Sir Ian Hamilton arrived and it was announced that he was going to review us. Our hopes rose. Sir Ian's reputation was high: it stood second only to that of General French among commanders in the field; and he would not have been sent here, we argued, to take charge of a minor operation. We guessed darkly at a big move contemplated. But still some said that we should not be used except as reserves. When others had broken the way for us we might be pushed in.

As I am writing this book entirely from memory, I cannot recall exactly how long elapsed between the review and the breaking of our camp at Mena. About a fortnight, I should think. The last event of our stay in Egypt had something of retributive justice in it; and it brought the Egyptian chapter to a dramatic end.

I refer to what all Australians know as the battle of the Wazzir; the Wazzir being that part of the city where most of the European prostitutes lived. There are various tales as to how the trouble arose: all that one can say with any certainty is that it was not premeditated. But the cause is not of importance: what was of some importance to Cairo was the result.

Australians have always had the blame (or the credit) of this affair, but the New Zealanders were equally concerned in it; and one story gives the origin of it to a New Zealander. The first sign of a fraças was a rush made by a number of soldiers on a certain house in the Wazzir, which was followed by the casting of its furniture into the street. It must then have occurred to the men that a thorough cleaning-up of the district was a duty that cried for performance. Another house was gutted in the same manner, and the self-appointed purifiers went on to a third. Word of what was happening spread apace, and Australasians gathered from all parts of the town. The hour was between 8 and 9 p.m., when men on pass were plentiful. With great speed every house in the street was emptied, and fire was set to the chattels.

By this time the military police were on the spot, but their efforts to quell the riot were ineffectual. Hoses were brought into play and were promptly cut, while the good work went on merrily. The Brass Hats were now alarmed, and some Territorial companies were marched to the scene. By the time they arrived the purification of the Wazzir was pretty complete.

It must have been with relief that General Birdwood received his orders to embark us; but as to this affair, a British officer in the Egyptian Service remarked that the purging of the Wazzir was the best thing that had happened to Cairo for years, and that the Australians deserved the thanks of the community and of the British Government.

Next day my battalion received its marching orders; by noon of the day following we had struck tents. A razed city is not more melancholy than a razed camp where men have lived for long, and that scene of desolation is with me yet. We sat on our kits until ordered to load them on the wagons, when most of us looked our last upon them. I

never saw mine again, and in losing it lost my South
African medal and discharges. The kits were to go no
further than Alexandria, but we were prepared to part
with them, and all that we urgently needed was in our
packs. At four we paraded: it was like saying good-bye
to a ruined home. Until then I did not know that the
place had been a home.

The 3rd Brigade was already embarked, and we, alone
of the 1st and 2nd Brigades, were now to join it. As we
marched past the lines of the 3rd, the 2nd and the 1st
Battalions, hundreds of men turned out from the tents to
cheer us. Proud to be leaving before them, we charitably
consoled them with the hope that they would not be far
behind us. The pipes were with the transport, but the
pipe band of the 5th Battalion was with us and played us
out of camp.

The cabs at the tram terminus by Mena House must
have called up many memories of jolly excursions, for we
had been partial to cabs when money was plentiful. We
did not know exactly where we were going, but we knew
that we were going on a very different sort of excursion
now. The sun was low, and the tree-shadowed road was
cool as we swung along it. The green fields of the fellaheen looked very green. Trams, cabs, motor-cars, native
policemen on white Arab stallions, camels loaded with
forage, bullock-carts loaded with women, all the life of the
Mena Road was sliding by us for the last time. We were
marching at ease, but there was not very much conversation. There was something very peaceful in the evening

light, and the moment was one for reflection. We had our last sight of the Pyramids just as the sun was setting. They shone pink.

Half-way to Cairo our friends of the 5th Battalion left us, and marched back to the camp which would know us no more. We tramped on in deepening silence as night fell. Kasr-el-Nil Barracks and Kasr-el-Nil Bridge dropped behind us, and we passed through the suburbs and entered the thickly-peopled streets of Cairo. On either hand faces appeared at windows; hundreds stood by the side of the road to look at us; but no one spoke; there was no sound at all, except of our feet tramping. The order to march at attention had extinguished such little talk as there had been.

We halted in the railway-station yard, piled arms and waited. We had rations with us, and we ate. It was a gloomy sort of business, eating biscuits in the dark; and the lights of Cairo beckoned. Having taken stock of the position, I slipped out of an unguarded gate and made for the nearest tavern. Here I found a man of my company who had had the same thought. We had a drink together. He was a young lawyer. I can't remember ever seeing him again. I know he was killed shortly after the landing.

We hurried back, in case the battalion should be en-training. We might have spared our haste. It was close upon midnight before we entrained. The men had by then found their tongues, and it was a rather noisy journey. But in any case no one could have slept, packed as we were on the uncushioned seats of third-class carriages. From the train we had merely to walk across the wharf to our transport, which was called the *Lake Michigan*.

The sun was high; there was no sign of breakfast, and we grew hungry. Inquiry of a ship's officer elicited the news that we were likely to sail the next morning. I and three of my tent-mates took counsel. We had never seen the inside of Alexandria. The temptation to view the city was great, especially as we might not have another chance of viewing any city. There was no guard or picket on the wharf; all was confusion on board; we seized the opportunity.

A fatigue party was working on the wharf, and we had simply to walk down the gangway as if we were members of the party or had been sent to join it. Before we were quite away we heard a call. Glancing back out of the corner of my eye, I made out my company commander, who had evidently spotted us. We filed behind a small mountain of stores and left the wharf under cover of it.

We were soon sitting down to a good breakfast in a café of the port. Presently some American bluejackets came in and started a conversation with us. One of them was a petty officer, and he showed a decided bias against the British. We were not looking for trouble, but we were not disposed to let trouble look for us; so one of us sat down at a piano and played 'God Save the King.' The rest of us, of course, rose and saluted. Equally of course the Americans stuck to their chairs.

Very civilly we pointed out to the petty officer that Egypt was a British protectorate, and that we expected foreigners to observe our customs here. One of these customs was to salute our national anthem. It would be played once more, and we hoped that they would oblige us.

The Americans were just equal to us in numbers, but the petty officer was the only one among them who looked at all formidable. His three subordinates were callow youths. He saw reason and called his men to attention as our pianist's fingers descended again upon the keyboard.

After that we filled their glasses and they filled ours, and we parted from them in amity.

We then set out on our survey of Alexandria. The streets were full of French soldiers, many of them in the picturesque uniforms of the Zouave, the Spahi and the Chasseur d'Afrique. We had a good day and arrived back at the quayside about four o'clock.

But it was not the same part of the quayside as we had left. Our transport was not to be seen, and none of the native bystanders knew anything about her. At length we spied a vessel on the opposite side of the harbour which we thought was she; this vessel was getting up steam, and to reach her by way of the wharves might, it seemed, take us an hour or two. To go by water would be quicker. We were close to some steps where small boats were lying, and without consulting the boatman we bundled into one of them.

Apparently it was built to carry two passengers, for he protested loudly at the third and passionately at the fourth. Heedless of him we pushed off, and pointed out the ship to which we desired to go.

His fears, however, were well founded, for the boat was not five yards from the steps when it settled and filled. Striking out, we regained the steps.

Very luckily for us an English officer was passing by at the moment, and our dripping forms attracted his attention. Inquiry into the circumstances of the accident informed him that we had set out to reach the *Lake Michigan*; whereupon he remarked that our best route was by land, as she was not three hundred yards away. Invisible though she was, this was the case; and we were aboard in five minutes.

We underwent a good deal of chaff about this escapade, but authority overlooked it. Our company commander was as conscientious an officer as we had, but he was also a very good fellow. I wish I could write of him in the present tense. He was killed in France while commanding the 56th Battalion.

§ 3

Nothing of interest marked the voyage to Lemnos. The food was rank, the meat sometimes uneatable, but there were few complaints about it. With the coming of embarkation orders the temper of the men had changed. Sick parades, which in Egypt had been largely attended, now drew no more than two or three to the doctor's shop Malingering had ceased altogether, and men who were really unwell refrained from reporting the fact, for fear of being landed somewhere or sent back to Egypt.

The isles of the Aegean were a disappointment to me.

Their bare green hills and scanty groves did not present the surpassing beauty which I had anticipated, and I was reminded that the Greeks, who had started the fuss about them, had never seen the islands of the South Seas.

The fine land-locked harbour of Lemnos was not without its charm, and here we came into the midst of a great fleet. We had travelled hither alone, and were surprised to find so large a company assembled. Day by day it grew.

There were merchantmen, tankers, and warships of every description: battleships as modern as the *Queen Elizabeth* and as ancient as the old barbette models of the French. Some of these last, with their vast target expanse and grotesque superstructure, were genuine curiosities of naval architecture, and much wonder was expressed that they were still in existence.

We were exercised on shore and in boat practice. Rowing classes provided amusement, particularly to onlookers in other ships. As we had to row in full marching order, rowing drill was hard work.

But the hardest exercise of all was the climbing of the rope ladders on the ship's side. Descending them was not easy, as the weight of our packs caused the ladders to bulge in the middle, so that sometimes we were clinging to them in an almost horizontal posture. Climbing them was an acrobatic feat which needed strength as well as skill. It seemed to us unnecessary, since our job, as we understood it, was to make a landing, not to land and retire. With full pack and haversack, rifle, bayonet, trenching-tool, water-bottle, and three hundred rounds of ammunition apiece, we had a weight of nearly seventy pounds distributed about us.

The information we had was that we were to land somewhere on the enemy's coast and that we might expect 40 per cent of casualties in effecting the operation. This was not read out in orders, but seemingly it was intended for general consumption, as the officers gave it out publicly to their men.

Beyond feeling that we had been honoured and should not fail, I don't think we thought much about it.

The next news was official and was read out in orders. This time there was no estimate of expected casualties. Having effected a landing, we were, it appeared, to march through the enemy's country. We were cautioned that those who fell out might fall into the enemy's hands, with, it was parenthetically added, unpleasant consequences. Our movements were likely to be so rapid that our transport would have to be left behind, so that it was incumbent upon us to carry all we were able to carry, and not to lighten our loads by throwing away rations, etc. It might be three days before our transport would overtake us, we were told. The lives and property of civilians were to be respected, and we were to be wary of the water. Particular attention was to be paid to the state of our feet.

We gathered from all this that we were in for a long and rapid march, and men who had been untroubled by the '40 per cent of casualties,' groaned at the thought of staggering onward for days under loads less fit for men than for horses. Constantinople again loomed as our

208

destiny; but instead of being landed at Constantinople we were to walk there.

The last order read to us at Lemnos was Sir Ian Hamilton's stirring charge to his army. We had then been three weeks at an anchor, and most of the fleet was still at an anchor when we sailed.

It was late in the afternoon. There was great enthusiasm on the ships past which we steamed. We might have been coming from a victory. The crews of the French warships were the most excited, but British restraint also quite broke down, for we saw two young officers dance a hornpipe on the deck of an English cruiser. I had not thought that the Navy could be so demonstrative, however moving the occasion.

Soon the green hills of Lemnos lay behind us, and dusk settled on the water.

CHAPTER XV

★

§ I

UP till now there had been little excitement among us, and one would have expected a degree of calm on the eve of battle; but this night there was pandemonium between decks. All lights were out, and men seemed to vie with one another as to who could make the most noise. They sang and yelled and catcalled, and nothing would quiet them. It was very disagreeable for those who wished to sleep; and one could not blame the man who called out in a clear voice during a moment's silence: 'Go your hardest. It's your last night on earth, my beauties!' The remark was received with hoots and cockadoodling. Thrice the adjutant tried to subdue the uproar, but it recommenced as soon as his back was turned. It was, in the circumstances, as strange an ebullition as I have ever witnessed, and was without parallel in my experience of soldiering.

The disturbance died down about eleven o'clock, and we slept till three in the morning, when we were roused and ordered to get ready. We had few preparations to make, and having added the last touches to the set of our packs, we went on deck.

We were steaming slowly past a dark and hilly coast where not a light was visible. The night was utterly quiet, the water black and calm. We had breakfast, and about half-past four heard the sound of distant rifle-fire. We steamed steadily on.

We had been told that we were to be in the first landing-

party, and were puzzled that the ball should have opened before our arrival.

The rifle-fire continued and increased, and was soon punctuated by gun-fire. Day was now breaking. Lights were twinkling on the coast, and before long we saw the flash of the guns. Other vessels, hidden hitherto by the darkness, began to reveal themselves.

We came to a standstill opposite a bluff-like hill, with a jumble of hills behind and on both sides of it. We watched with interest a battery to our right, which was firing shell after shell at strings of boats and lighters loaded with troops, which were being towed ashore by tugs and launches. In the growing light we were able to see everything clearly. The *Triumph* and another warship were near us and were replying to the Turkish battery, whose shells were throwing up fountains about the boats. Occasionally they threw up more than a fountain. The ends of a boat would suddenly rise in the air like a closing pair of scissors, and a cluster of khaki-clad figures be scattered in the water. Some were picked up, some were not. Presently the *Triumph* ran close inshore and re-engaged the battery. It was less active after that. The *Triumph's* fire seemed very accurate, and some of her shells must certainly have found their mark.

Naval launches were buzzing about everywhere, and the scene was one of the liveliest commotion. The sun came out very brightly, as if to grace a festival, and indeed there was something very festive in the aspect of the sparkling blue water and the animated craft upon it. I had a difficulty in realizing that this was war: it was so much like a regatta. I was reminded of Sydney harbour on a fine morning, with the ferry-boats darting about and the liners at anchor. A waterspout that rose alongside us cleared my head of fancies; a big gun somewhere in the background was getting our range. We discreetly changed position.

But the knowledge that we were something more than spectators could not rob the display of its strong theatrical interest, and as long as I looked at it I saw it as a thrilling panorama.

Among its details, the midshipmen in the launches took my eye. They were having the time of their lives, smoking enormous pipes (or pipes which appeared enormous in their mouths) and talking and generally comporting themselves as if they were at Henley. If only their mothers could have seen them on that day! Their competence and composure must have contributed in no small measure to the success of the landing. Some were mere children, as one could tell not only by their appearance but by their voices.

Our turn to take the stage came at half-past seven. By this time every other battalion of the 1st, 2nd and 3rd Brigades was ashore, and we were cast for the part of divisional reserve. Whether this was due to an accident or to a change in the original arrangements I never learned. I rather think that it was an accident and that the landing, as planned, was to have taken place near where we were when the firing started.

By orders, we had loosened our equipment, in such a manner that we could slip out of it in a moment if the boat were smashed or swamped. The gun-fire was now much less, however, and all our boats got ashore in safety, towed in strings of four or five by the launches. As we neared the shore the launches cast off and we pulled in. The beach was already a dressing-station and a mortuary. We marched past a long line of dead, and a youth beside me turned rather green at the sight of them. He said something – I forget what – but it was an expression of horror – as if this sight were totally unexpected. I had been impressed by his insouciance up till that moment. I guessed now that he had no imagination, that he had never attempted to envisage the facts of war, or his view of those dead might have sickened but would not have shocked him.

The colonel and his staff had been the first to land, and, followed by A Company, we had moved off to the right along the beach, until we came to a gully, up which we struck. I have said that we were in reserve, and our services were not at present required. Headquarters stayed at the bottom of the gully, and the companies marched up it. We were pretty snug here, although shrapnel soon began to burst above our heads. A Turkish airman had marked us. However, the guns never quite got on to us, and we suffered only one casualty, a lieutenant wounded. A company commander climbed a little way up the hill, to get a view of the fleet, and descended very hurriedly. A shell that burst on the beach had narrowly missed him.

213

His facial expression was very comical, and the colonel chaffed him mildly. Wounded came down the gully from time to time, and gave us reports of the fighting. All were in good spirits, and some were very unwilling to go aboard ship. According to their accounts our men were doing well.

We lunched, and at three in the afternoon an officer was sent to the top of the gully, to discover, if possible, how matters were going in the firing-line. He returned with the report that the battle appeared to be rolling back to us. This we had noticed, from the louder sound of the rifle-fire. I judged that it would not be long before we were wanted, and my forecast was speedily verified.

Our armourer-sergeant, who was battalion runner, arrived from brigade headquarters with our orders. I carried the word back to our companies and made haste to rejoin the colonel, who by this time was leading the battalion along the beach. On my way down I passed General Bridges, our divisional commander, looking very ungeneral-like. He was dressed in slacks and shirt and a plain cap, and wore no insignia whatever. His equipment consisted of a haversack and a pair of field-glasses. But his height and the very plainness of his outfit made him a conspicuous figure, so that, as he was always too ready to expose himself, it was no wonder that he was killed.

Having marched for a short distance along the beach, in the direction we had first taken, we turned once more to our left and proceeded inland. The path was fairly good, and led us through what was afterwards known as

Shrapnel Gully. The sky had become clouded, and the wild, scrubby hills were dark and dreary. The sound of the firing grew very distinct, and before we had gone far we came under shell-fire. The Turkish airmen were doing good work.

At a little plateau we halted and took off our packs. Our way from this point went steeply upwards, and we had to lighten our loads if we were to make the haste required of us. The plateau was well covered by fire, but we made our dash across it without accident. Many wounded had passed us, and about this point we saw many who were not wounded. They wore the colours of almost every battalion in the Division, but we had not time to ask them what they were doing here. We knew afterwards that they were skulkers from the firing-line.

The hillside gave us partial protection from the shrapnel, but some of the shells burst close enough. One nearly got our senior major, who was immediately ahead of me. His cap flew off and he dropped to his knees and clapped his hands to his head. The colonel turned anxiously round at the major's loud exclamation. He was unhurt, but the shock dazed him for a few minutes, and he stumbled on, talking so wildly and despondently that I feared that his brain was affected. No doubt, for the moment it was. Later he was to achieve a glorious record which made one of the most astonishing stories of the war.

From this steep part of the path we came, round an elbow of the hill, to a level stretch; and here, as we had outstripped the battalion and the fire was much less troublesome, the colonel halted. We sat down by the wayside. The lowering sky, the desolate, sombre, savage terrain about us made the strongest possible contrast with the bright panorama of the morning. In a minute or two A Company came up with us. High above the path, among the bushes, a staff officer appeared and shouted directions, and A Company went ahead. One platoon scuttled past us, being under the odd impression that this was a danger point.

We stayed. There was no appearance of B Company. I was sitting next to the colonel, and I heard him remark that B Company was a long time. B was my company, and I asked him if I might go and hurry them up; for I could not imagine what was delaying them, unless they had lost the way. I received permission and went. Although the fire was still hot round the corner, I was glad to be doing something. I had not gone far before I met B Company, which pushed on more rapidly when I had delivered my message. Continuing, I came on a platoon which was taking a track that branched out of the main track. Where they – and those who followed them – would have arrived is more than I can say, but I should think they would probably have been lost, as the trend of the path was away from our battle line.

Near the bottom of the hill I came on a company resting! They had, it appeared, lost touch with the column, and were uncertain of the way. This was the rear company, and having directed them I returned. Altogether, my effort had not been wasted. Climbing the hill a second time was toilsome work, but I had a sense of satisfaction which made me oblivious both to fatigue and to the heavy fire. What struck me as most curious about this affair was that few of the officers seemed to realize that any haste was needed. More than one questioned the authenticity of my orders, and seemed to think that I was exaggerating the state of the case.

What had happened was that the landing troops had been cut to bits, and were clinging with the utmost difficulty to the heights they had won. The need of fresh troops in the line could not have been more urgent. But nearly all our officers were new to war.

Battalion headquarters had completed the ascent of the hill when I rejoined them, and taken up a position just below the ridge. The last bit of the way was the roughest and steepest, and I was not sorry to rest. On the other side of the ridge the battalion was starting to entrench itself. By evening it was dug in, and the second-in-command, quite recovered, had taken charge of the line.

We were all very thirsty, but our desert training stood us in good stead, and we knew better than to empty our water-bottles, filled on the ship last evening. Some men had no rations, having unwisely stowed them in their packs (their haversacks being heavy with the extra ammunition we were carrying), so those who had food shared with those who had not. None of us had overcoats, and we missed them, as rain fell later on and the night was cold. About ten o'clock we had a visitor. Colonel (afterwards General Sir Charles) Rosenthal, of the artillery, had found his way up, guideless, in the dark, to inquire where we wanted the guns posted. It was not his fault that the guns were still on the beach the next afternoon. The only guns we had in position during the first two days were those of an Indian mountain battery, which performed good but hardly adequate service.

There was heavy firing at intervals through the night, and we expected hourly to be rushed, but the enemy held off, for some inscrutable reason. He could have rushed us with ease, our line being so thin that he could have broken it anywhere. He contented himself with shouting abuse and taunts at us and calling upon Allah. These cries coming from the darkness sounded weirdly. One of the enemy, a German probably, called out in very good English: 'Come on, Australians, and show yourselves! You aren't in the Wazzir now!' So news of that little affair must have travelled far.

Notwithstanding these disturbances and the rain, I had a little fitful sleep, which refreshed me.

The morning was fairly quiet. Some snipers annoyed us; bullets licked the stones and flew overhead, but none of us at headquarters was hit. A wounded man was brought in about nine o'clock. He belonged to another battalion, and told how he had lain out with five others since yesterday afternoon and had seen his comrades bayoneted by a party of Turks. He himself had escaped by shamming dead, and had been hours — he could not tell how long — crawling in to us. We made him as comfortable as we could till a stretcher party bore him off.

A lieutenant of the 3rd Brigade was the next to drop in. He had lost his battalion and seemed to be greatly afflicted in mind. He was inexpressibly haggard – gray and ghastly. He sat for a minute with his chin in his hands. He had landed, he said, with the first landing party, and had been fighting through the whole of yesterday. He had then gone with a message to another battalion and had lost his way in returning.

The colonel told him where he was likely to find his battalion, and he dragged himself to his feet and tottered off.

A party was sent down to bring our packs up. Mine was not found, which was annoying, as I had a pound of tobacco in it. Mules arrived with boxes of ammunition, and, what pleased us more, some carriers came with water. We drank what was left in our bottles and refilled them.

Our wounded were dribbling past in no great numbers. Most of them were walking, but we heard of a good many men who could not be moved, on account of a shortage of stretchers. Among these was the commander of my platoon, who had been badly wounded in the groin. He passed us about midday, suffering cheerfully, and died on his way to Egypt.

The sun was shining again, and the day was as hot as last night had been cold. The *Queen Elizabeth* fired continually over our heads, her great shells passing so close as to give us painful tremors. I imagine that a few days of this would have been enough to set up shell-shock. We were much more worried by it than by the enemy's fire, and everybody complained. We must have been in direct line with the target, for the shells seemed to pass within a few feet of our heads. The effect was purely physical; we were not in the least afraid that a shell would drop among us; though it did happen that the *Queen Elizabeth* wiped out some of our men.

A friend of mine, sent on an errand, stopped for a chat with me, and told me of an experience he had had this morning. He had gone behind the lines, to wash in a puddle, when two officers of another battalion seized him. I must tell you that it was a fancy of his to shave his head; and, having been washing his face, he had his hat off. Seeing his shaved head, the officers jumped to the conclusion that he was a Turk; a revolver was pointed at him, and nothing but his Australian accent saved his life.

This panicky action had some excuse, for several Turks and Germans, dressed in our uniform, had been found in our lines. One was even discovered and arrested on the beach; another had brought an order to retire, and the order was about to be executed, when one of our officers suspected something. He at once put the question: 'What transport did you come to Egypt in?' The bogus Australian was stumped, and was shot where he stood. All these men, I heard, died bravely; but that, of course, is not surprising, as they must have been brave men.

About 3 p.m. an order came. The battalion was to advance.

There was something very queer about that order. It was vague to the last degree. I am not sure if the order was 'advance' or 'attack,' but I am pretty sure that no objective was mentioned. The colonel appeared not to understand it, but his hesitation was summarily cut short by the discovery that the troops were leaving their trenches! Seemingly the men had received the order before it reached the colonel.

We at once hopped out after them.

My memories of the next hour or so are clear but incoherent. I have never been able to form a rational picture either of what we were doing or of what we were intended to do. I found myself with the colonel, the adjutant, the signalling officer, several signallers and others. We ran, stopping occasionally in abandoned trenches. Machine guns and rifles played briskly on us. Once, when we had halted behind some bushes, the signalling officer, who was beside me, gave a loud grunt, and said he was hit in the leg. I was only surprised that we weren't all hit, as a machine gun had got the range of our party nicely. We left the signalling officer in an abandoned trench. His wound was not serious, and he was able to resume duty before the evening. He was then shot through the head.

Owing to the broken nature of the ground, we had lost sight of the troops; but their cheers as they charged told us of their whereabouts. Twice or three times we heard those thin, high cheers. We passed a great many dead. The majority were Australians. In one spot were half a dozen. Though last night's rain must have washed them, they looked curiously dusty. One man was kneeling on one knee; his head was slightly bowed over his rifle, which he still grasped; its butt rested on the ground. Until I looked at his face I thought that he was alive. It astonished me that he should have died and stiffened in this attitude.

Imperceptibly our small party disintegrated, and at last I was alone with the colonel. A man wearing the colours of the 5th Battalion joined us. He seemed to spring up from nowhere. The air sang with bullets, and in running we crouched as low as we could, and lay on our bellies frequently.

I had some strange fancies. The most persistent of them was that this was a field-day; that presently the 'Cease Fire' would sound, and we should march back to camp and the canteen – the canteen and beer! Beer! My thirst was such that I could have drunk a gallon of beer at a draught.

Topping a rise, we came in sight of a hillock on the slope of which a number of men were lying. We distinguished the colours of many battalions including our own green-and-white. One of the green-and-whites raised his hand to us. It was the major; with him was the adjutant and the corporal of signallers.

We joined them.

All but ourselves of the Fourth were men who had been separated from their battalions and were fighting the Turks independently. Colonel Thompson took them under his command. They were a very game lot and behaved like veterans.

Although the hill covered us from the front, we must have been seen gathering there, for shells began to burst over our heads as the colonel and I arrived. They came in fours pretty regularly. We were also being somewhat annoyed by a couple of snipers, one of whom, on our left, I saw for an instant. I was about to try for a shot at him when another quartette of shells caused me to lie low. One – Two – Three: each burst nearer to me than its predecessor: I had a dull conviction that my hour was striking. It struck.

There was a crash, right in my ears; and something hit me with stunning force on the head. I believed that I was killed, and my thought was: 'Well, that's the end of it!' I had no fear. In the very presence of death there is no room for fear, no room for any emotion.

Then I realized that I was not dead; and I became at the same time aware of a great pain in my right wrist. I forgot all about my head wound; the pain in my wrist absorbed me. I lifted my arm, and the pain increased to agony. The hand hung like the end of a broken stick; it was almost severed.

The corporal rummaged for my field dressings.

The colonel was concerned about my head wound. Blood was streaming from it and it appeared much worse than it was. I told him that it was nothing, but that my arm was broken.

When the wound had been roughly dressed, the colonel said I had better get back to the lines, and pointed out my route to me.

I did not demur, for I knew that with one arm I was useless here; and the pain was now very great.

I picked up my hat and rifle and made off.

I was in the dip between the little hill and the rise we had crossed when I heard shouts of 'Unfix your bayonet!' The sun was shining, and the glittering bayonet made me a mark; and no doubt the men behind me saw that I was drawing fire. But with one hand I could not unfix my bayonet as I ran; to stop would have been suicidal; and the idea of dropping my rifle never entered my head.

I ran, or, rather, lurched and stumbled on, weak in the knees and giddy; and stopped for a few minutes in some cover where I found a knot of our men. They were well sheltered, and strongly advised me to stay; but the pain of the dangling member was intolerable, and I would have taken any risks rather than suffer it a minute longer than I must. One of the men unfixed my bayonet for me, and I set out once more.

I had now to cross a comparatively level expanse. I have said that the air sang with bullets as the colonel and I went forward; I can find no word to express what the fire was like now. It appeared to come from every direction but that I was taking. I could no more than walk, and I could not crouch or I should have fallen. A bullet creased the bridge of my nose, and another banged on my trenching-tool. My haversack was shot through and my hat knocked off again. This time I let it lie. I was not concerned with hats. But I still held on to my rifle.

I had one idea in my mind: to reach a dressing-station.

I was in such excruciating agony that I hardly considered my poor chance of reaching anywhere. The whanging, wailing devil's orchestra became a conglomerate of sound and nothing more; it failed to penetrate to my fear-consciousness.

Its intensity decreased, as the roar of a mob dies down into the sound of single voices. I heard *bullets*. In front of me I saw trenches and men. Men standing, walking about, walking up to the trenches. As I came nearer to them I recognized men of my own company. They were on rising ground, which put this part of the field out of the fire zone.

The machine-gun officer, my platoon sergeant and several others spoke to me, and I passed on. I had picked up the lie of the land and I knew the way. It did not occur to me then to wonder why my company was back, and my colonel and his second-in-command still out there: but from this and the fact that the rest of the battalion was retiring or had already retired, you can judge of how this stunt had been conducted. The Fourth had gone out against an entire division, newly arrived, and had lost about a quarter of its strength in doing so. The Australians were paying dearly for experience. But in this first couple of days they had proved two things conclusively: that they could fight and that they could take punishment. Of the cunning and skill they were later to show they had given scarcely a sign.

Colonel Onslow Thompson, I may say here, never regained our lines. A shell took the top of his head off.

Half-way down the hill I came to a dressing-station. My arm was put in splints, firmly bandaged and slung, and the relief which this gave me was so great that my spirits rose to the highest pitch. The ambulance man insisted that I should leave my rifle, and I left it – with reluctance. He was not busy at the time, and he very kindly took me down to the beach – and possibly saved my life thereby, for the path was at places a death-trap, and he helped me to run when it was necessary to run, and guided me through the scrub at other dangerous points. On the way we met a number of lost sheep, whom I exhorted to rejoin their comrades. They took me, I think, for an officer: all, at any rate, started up the hill, and some perhaps arrived. My guide had bandaged my head and my nose and also a flesh wound in my left arm, of which I had been unaware, so that I appeared on the beach looking like a mummy in poor condition. An A.S.C. sergeant remarked that I seemed to have got away with more than my share, and there were other humorous comments.

I had to wait an hour or more for a boat, and while I sat by the shore an acquaintance joined me. He too was wounded, in the leg; it was not a bad wound and he was making a great fuss about being sent away. He could not see why he should not stay and be treated in the field hospital; but the Red Cross men were firm: all casualties had to be evacuated. He produced a full flask of Greek brandy, and I took a long pull at it. I must have drunk nearly a gill; but with one thing and another I was pretty done; and without hesitation I can state that it was the best drink I ever had. This Samaritan's name was Simpson; his brother was a captain of ours, his father the New South Wales Chief Judge in Equity. He recovered quickly from his wound, returned to the Peninsula, and, I am sorry to say, was killed.

The boat came along and we climbed into it and were pulled out to a steamer. It was now dark.

The steamer's gangway was down for walking cases, and I tried to walk up it, but failed, so they made me go up in the basket. This vexed me, seeing that I was not hit in the legs, and having walked down to the beach, had some right to consider myself a walking case. From the steamer's rail I tried to jump to the deck, but was caught in the act by two orderlies. The brandy had, doubtless, exhilarated me, but I was also, I think, exhilarated by the events of the day.

I slept soundly that night on an iron deck, and next morning found that there were many of my platoon aboard, including the sergeant, whose jaw a stray bullet had smashed shortly after he had spoken to me. I have forgotten the name of this ship: she was a transport and was still carrying horses (for our march) which went back to Alexandria with us. The hospital ships had been soon filled, and there was no choice but to put the wounded on transports.

Early in the morning we received the attention of the Turkish gunners, and had a bad five minutes before the engineers could get the ship under way. Having escaped death on shore, we earnestly desired to live a little longer, and had the ship been sunk there would have been no hope for us.

Having moved to a safer berth, we received some more boat-loads of wounded and sailed about midday.

The brandy had made me bleed profusely, so that my bandages were completely saturated. I must have looked a shocking sight, and had many respectful tributes paid to me. A young Queensland subaltern eyed me admiringly as I stood by the rail and watched the receding shore, thinking of those I had left.

'An old dog for a hard road!' he said.

Unshaven, bloody, begrimed, I probably appeared not less than fifty, instead of thirty-seven.

My arm was again becoming painful, but one of the surgeons advised me not to have it touched. They could not, he said, give it proper attention here, being overwhelmed with cases. This was true. The surgeons were incessantly employed in saving, or trying to save, the lives of the dangerously wounded. There were no cots, of course, nor even hammocks, and we slept side by side on sail-cloths spread on the iron plates.

The next night and the next I had no sleep at all. On the fourth night I spoke to an orderly and asked if I might have a sleeping-draught. I thought he could bring it without disturbing a doctor; but he fetched a doctor to me. I was given a hypodermic injection, and had scarcely concluded my apologies before I was dozing.

That night's sleep was of great benefit to me. It gave me rest from the constant discomfort of my arm, and put me in fair trim for Alexandria, where we arrived on the fifth day. A news-boy came aboard with Egyptian papers, and we read of our performances. These press notices were very flattering. We were distinctly pleased. We realized that we had done something, although privately aware that it might have been done in better style.

Ambulances ran us to a tented hospital, where we were inspected, bathed and dressed in 'blues.' The orderlies were collecting badges, and they took mine, when they had cut my tunic from me. I could have retained them, I suppose, but I was not caring much about badges.

After my bath I sat for a long time in a marquee with my back against a tent-pole. One by one my fellows were summoned away, and came back, cheerful, with their wounds dressed; and it seemed at last that I had been forgotten. An orderly was reminded of me; he said I had missed my turn and should have to wait till to-morrow. Weary though I was, I was not in a mood to abide quietly by this decision, and, accompanied by my sergeant, I sought a doctor. We found a very nice young fellow from Edinburgh, who gave me half an hour of his best attention. Cutting the congealed bandages off was a long job, the soakage of blood having stiffened them to the consistency of board. My arm was black, and I feared mortification, but the young man reassured me. He told me further that, though my soldiering days were done, I was not likely to lose the arm. The smash was complete, but the bones might be expected to knit in time.

He marked me for England.

CHAPTER XVI

★

§ 1

I SPENT a year in England; and I shall pass over that period with those words. The record of my hospital life would be dull; and though certain events of my private life were important to me, they are not of concern to the reader.

I sailed from England in April of 1916, unfit for further service, and after spending six weeks in Sydney, set out again for Tahiti.

Meredith was dead. He had survived the first week's fighting and been promoted to corporal and to sergeant; had received a mortal wound and died at sea. He was buried in the Aegean, a fitting grave for him.

Papeete I found less changed than I had expected. The damage from the German bombardment had been repaired, and the atmosphere of war was hardly perceptible here. One could easily have fancied that Tahiti lay in a world which no war troubled. Men spoke of it, but as of a distant thing; it had not coloured or darkened their existences.

After I had visited old friends, I called upon the manager of S. R. Maxwell & Co., the largest British trading company in the town. He was not sure if he could employ me, and consulted his director, Mr. J. L. Young. Mr. Young became interested, upon learning that I had been at the Gallipoli landing. His only son had been killed there.

A man was wanted, and all that was against me was my total inexperience of trading. I think that my war service turned the scale for me. The travelling manager, Captain 'Winnie' Brander, was called in; he consented to take me, and I was engaged.

Mr. Young was very kind, and carried me off to lunch with him at Lovaina's. Next day I sailed in the *Heitiare*, a sixty-ton schooner, for the Paumotu Archipelago.

Captain Brander commanded this vessel, and was most interesting company for me. He had known Stevenson and his family when they were in Tahiti, and Kitchener, while on his tour of the British Dominions, had lunched with him and his brothers. He was a cousin of my old employer Tauraa, and thus another nephew of the queen. A Frenchman by nationality, he was proud of the Scottish blood which came to him from his father, and was a shrewd critic of English, French and Tahitian character. One of his brothers had been a British midshipman; he himself had spent almost the whole of his life in Island trading.

We called at Makatea, Niau and Anaa before setting our course for Makemo. The first was a phosphate island, an atoll which some submarine disturbance had lifted out of the sea, giving it queer low cliffs and a dry lagoon. Its upheaval had left it a dead thing. It resembled a shallow bowl, and was a mournful sight; but it was rich and important: an object-lesson in man's criterion of values.

Niau and Anaa were as pleasing as Makatea was displeasing. To the inexperienced eye one atoll looks, at a distance, just like another. I have, in a novel,[1] described the sight, and I cannot give a better idea of it than by quoting that description:

'First was seen a long broken line of green on the sea's verge; then what appeared to be a chain of low islets clothed with palms: finally a continuous white beach showed itself as the basis of the whole delicate fabric, which had the appearance of some monstrous marine growth. Such, of course, essentially it was; but one could imagine it drifting away, or sinking without commotion beneath the water.'

Anaa has the peculiarity of a green lagoon. Against the intense ultramarine of the sea the effect of this emerald lake is very startling, as a strip of beach two hundred yards wide is all that divides it from the ocean. An atoll is one of the most singular sights in the world. It is simply a chain of coral, bare on its windward side where the sea frequently breaches it, and partly or wholly hedged with cocoanut-trees where the land has better protection. It is seldom anywhere more than a furlong wide, and most of it is much less; yet this tenuous girdle often holds a lagoon thirty miles in length.

At Anaa I was entertained by the local trader, a French Canadian who had served in the North-West Mounted Police. We drank luke-warm bottled beer in his thatched dining-room and were served by his wife, a native. She was not the shrinking half-wild creature commonly presented in South Sea stories as 'the trader's wife.' One did not wonder why he had married her or how he endured

[1] *The Game* (Geoffrey Bles).

this existence. Such wonder would have been not merely impertinent but contrary to reason, for he was as animated, hearty and obviously happy a man as you would meet in any land. His home had even a Dickensian tone of domesticity; but the further one goes afield the more analogous the world grows.

The voyage throughout was like a yachting cruise, for weather and balmy serenity. Not that it would have wholly delighted those to whom the suburban refinements are a need not to be dispensed with. The sanitary arrangements were simple, and, I may add, public; the cockroach was not absent, either from board or bed, and below deck one noticed an aroma of copra and engine-oil — for the schooner had an auxiliary engine for use in calms and in shooting lagoon passages. But there are some to whom such trifles give a tang to life, a sense of being closer to the realities, which refinement tends to smother.

We carried a mate (the captain's son), a half-caste engineer and a crew of Tahitians. Not the least of the ship's company was the cook, who was Captain Brander's discovery. Spending most of his time at sea, and having a proper regard for his digestion, he was particular about the *Heitiare's* cook.

The cabin and trade-room formed the only part of the vessel below deck which was not devoted to cargo. The trade-room was just abaft the cabin, from which it was divided by a wire screen. Here on shelves was stored everything in the way of merchandise (food excepted) which an Islander desires, from calico to electric torches.

The desire for the latter was not a want generated by snobbishness: nowhere is the electric torch more valuable than in the South Seas.

The trade wind blew steadily and gently, and the nights were even more placid than the days. This, mid-winter, was the halcyon time of the year. Occasionally a call would come from the deck at night, and the captain spring bare-footed up the companion-way. He seemed to sleep like a dog with one ear always cocked. There was need of that in these waters, the most treacherous in the seven seas. The innumerable low islands of the archipelago made navigation difficult, and the difficulty was greatly increased by the currents, which were strong and continually shifting. One evening, I remember, we were on deck. It was a quiet night of stars, and the sails were barely drawing. The creak of the blocks was the only sound to be heard besides our voices. Captain Brander seemed to grow uneasy. He rose from the locker where we were sitting, and walked to the port rail. He turned round to me and declared that he could smell land. There should have been no land just hereabouts, but the currents allowed of no certainty. We kept on and by and by a smudge appeared on the horizon. I could not see it until I had looked at it a long time; but there it was, an atoll. A current had carried us far out of our course.

§ 2

Makemo has a passage at each end of it, one to the east and one to the west: nearly all these islands lie north-east by south-west, and the group too follows this direction. We entered by the western passage, the further from the settlement. As the lagoon began to open out we saw a cutter approaching. She came alongside, and a middle-aged native of dignified appearance sprang aboard us. He was the chief of the island and a French magistrate; and he was also postmaster and pilot. It was in his rôle of pilot that he now appeared, and standing in the rigging he proceeded to con the schooner up the lagoon.

Reefs made the water a labyrinth, and it took us several hours to reach the settlement, which was situated at the far end of this great lagoon. To port we could see the ocean plainly through the gaps in the cocoanut groves, and sometimes between the trees: to starboard, seven or eight miles off, was the bare reef. A marine lake is a good descriptive epithet for the smooth expanse of water we were traversing. Although we were actually encompassed by land, we were much more truly encompassed by deep water.

We moored not far from the wharf, and Captain Brander and I went ashore in the whaleboat. There was considerable stir on shore. Furniture, stores and bagged copra were being conveyed to the wharf, and it seemed as if all the inhabitants not thus employed had turned out to greet us. We were met by the man whose place I was for the next six months to fill. He was going to Hikueru, where the pearling season was about to open, and was taking with him all the divers of the island, their wives, families and belongings. When the Polynesian travels he takes home with him. To leave his wife would be, in his view, foolish and rash, a wife being no less necessary abroad than at home, and, unless under one's eye, insecure property. The woman's point of view is rather similar, and she has, moreover, a liking for travel.

Captain Brander was to sail next morning for Hikueru, with such cargo as was ready for him, and return in three or four days' time for the trader, so I had to pick up the threads of the business quickly. South Sea trading is quite a specialized branch of commerce, and had I served an apprenticeship to a grocer, it might not, in the present undertaking, have been much to my advantage. It may, in fact, have been an advantage to me that I knew nothing whatever of trade. I had, I mean, nothing to unlearn.

My instruction was interrupted on the first day by what was, for me, an embarrassing and utterly unexpected occurrence. In Tahiti the war had seemed a remote matter; here, perhaps because of its remoteness, and the fact that I was the first person who had come from it, I was an interesting and distinguished figure in the popular eye.

It was hastily decided that a banquet was the proper form of welcome to me, and as it was impossible for me to refuse it, I found myself, at four o'clock in the afternoon, for the first time in my life a Guest of Honour. To make matters worse, the captain and Jacobi the trader were too busy to attend the feast, so that I was left quite unsupported.

We sat down at a long table in the chief's house, after

all the notables, including the policeman, had been presented to me. Girls of the household waited, and I was crowned with flowers. Now, I am really a modest man, despite these memoirs.

There was abundance of wine and I gained some courage from it. For an hour and a half we ate and drank, and then came the most dreaded ordeal, the speech-making. I was given an address, unilluminated but neatly written on a sheet torn out of a ledger (I have it still) and to this I had to reply. The address was in Tahitian, and as few of the company had any knowledge of English or more than a smattering of French, I had to reply in Tahitian. I had never learned to speak this language well, and it was nearly four years since I had used it daily: add to that I am a naturally diffident speaker and had never before delivered a speech to a gathering; and the fact that these people listened with the gravest attention will give you some idea of the excellence of their manners. There was not the semblance of a smile on any face; not a hint that they did not understand me perfectly, that I was not indeed the most fluent and lucid of orators.

I sat down to applause, and another guest rose. Others followed and I spoke once more in reply, but by that time the wine had done its work, and my tongue was at least fluent. I mixed English, French and Tahitian in a most wonderful oration. We concluded by singing the *Marseillaise* and *Tipperary* (Tahitian version). By many Polynesians *Tipperary* was, I think, believed at that time to be our national anthem.

237

Notwithstanding these amenities, an incident occurred late that night which showed the fierce and changeable temper of these people. On account of some supposed offence to the chief, three of his young men broke into our compound and attempted to assault Jacobi. They were expelled; an apology was sent in the morning, and explanations were exchanged.

The chief was to go with the pearlers; and at parting he made me a present of a pair of black-lipped pearl-shells.

§ 3

Makemo, the village, was so small, and so simply constituted, that it can be brought to the reader's eye in a few lines. Its most prominent landmark was the white town hall on the edge of the lagoon, built of coral by the inhabitants, without the aid of architects or masons. Opposite it, on the street which ran from the wharf to the ocean beach, was the residence of Maxwell & Co.'s representative. It was a tiny wooden bungalow of three rooms, with front and back verandahs. Nearer the lagoon and on the other side of a gate stood the warehouse, and next to it the copra-house, and behind them was the store or shop, a square, high-peaked edifice, roofed with shingles, surrounded by a verandah and connected by a covered way with an office. The store faced the eastern passage, a hundred yards wide, and a road of beaten coral alongside it; residence, warehouse, copra-house and store were all enclosed in a white-washed paling fence. The yard thus formed contained several cocoanut-trees, but was other-

wise as bare as a barrack square. Following the road beside the passage, which skirted a cocoanut grove and gave
access to a number of palm-leaf huts and small cottages,
one came to the ocean beach. The ocean beach was as
different from the lagoon beach as a man's face is from a
girl's; as rugged as the other was smooth, as severe as the
other was mild. This was no beach for the holiday-maker;
it was iron-bound, to receive the long white combers
which the world's greatest ocean rolled upon it. There
was hardly a smooth yard of it. It was almost like the
time-worn ruins of a city, it was so fantastically piled with
rocks and boulders.

The road turning sharply to the left here, made a pro-
menade for it; and turning to the left once more, one
entered the main street.

This was shaded, all its length, by cocoanut-trees, and
lined by low garden walls of coral. The dwellings ranged
from the cocoanut-leaf shanty to the cottage of wood and
iron. The church was of coral, built by its flock, and coral
was the material of some of the old houses. Modern taste
was setting, alas! towards American wood and corrugated
iron. The palm-leaves to some extent hid and softened
these horrors. One tried to forget them. At the end of the
street were the hall, the wharf and the flag-staff, where
none but the French flag was allowed to fly.

Such was the village of Makemo, which one could
walk round in fifteen minutes. It was tidy and clean, not
through striving to be so, but by virtue of an innate bent
which some people have. But perhaps I am praising where

praise is not due. There were no newspapers on Makemo (but those the mail brought), no paper bags and no ready-made cigarettes. Thus there could not be the untidiness of England.

After Jacobi left, there were three white men besides myself on the island: a Frenchman, a Dane and a Chilian, or Chileno, as the last was called. He was not exactly white, but he was white by courtesy. The Frenchman was a huge old man-o'-war's-man, whose consumption of vinegar at first astonished me. He used to come daily to the store for a pint bottle of it. I remarked on this to the Dane, who was my next-door neighbour, and heard the explanation. The wine-cellar was empty; to eat one's breakfast or dinner without at least an illusion of *vin ordinaire* was impossible; so, to escape starvation, vinegar had been substituted. My vinegar was a first-class article, and possibly just as suitable for a beverage as much of the wine that is sold. The old *matelot* did not stay long with us. He sailed one day in a cutter for Hikueru, with a native, the native's wife, their two children, three pigs and a family of fowls. The cutter was old and leaky, but somehow she reached the pearling island, where wine and rum were plentiful.

Other substitutes than vinegar for strong drink were sometimes used on Makemo. I had in stock a French neuralgia and tooth-ache cure, called Alcoöl de Menthe. It was highly spirituous and, mixed with water, not very palatable, but cocoanut-water made it not too harsh to be relished by the determined drinker. Throughout the

Archipelago, which, as I have elsewhere observed, was a 'dry' area, this mixture was known as a Paumotu cock-tail: I have drunk it on schooners as an *apéritif*, and a single glass of it can be taken without apparent harm. The sale of Alcoöl de Menthe was restricted; the trader could not sell it to a native, and had to be satisfied that it was wanted for medicinal purposes. I found neuralgia and tooth-ache extraordinarily prevalent.

My neighbour the Dane was an old merchant-seaman, who had settled twenty years ago on Makemo and married the late chief's daughter. By her he had three children, a boy and two girls. All were good-looking; the elder girl dark, small and vivacious; the younger fair, with bright brown hair, and very pretty; the boy (he was a young man of twenty-one) handsome in a melancholy style, but rather characterless. Their father had once been a trader, but Maxwell's had extinguished him, and he now lived on the proceeds of his wife's inheritance, a large tract of cocoanut land. He did not enjoy idleness; though he was sixty he had an ambition to go to sea again, and was one of the few old Southseamen I have met who appeared alien to their surroundings. The process of assimilation which usually takes place had not taken place in him; he remained in every fibre of him a Dane. In settling in these isles he had obeyed not an instinct but a fancy: he knew that now, but he had learned the truth too late in the day. He was not popular with the natives, who considered him cranky; he was a stranger even in his family. We talked often at night on his verandah, and his thoughts seemed always to turn to Denmark and the sea. He had the crab-like walk of the traditional seaman; the forward stance, the loosely pendant arms; one pictured him on a sloping and slippery deck. He had not even a hobby for a solace. He owned a cutter, in which he might have sailed and fished, but he had given it up to his son, who was married and lived at the other end of the lagoon. He read novels and gossiped and lamented his fate. When physical inaction became intolerable, he would walk round the settlement as round a race-track. As lap after lap was completed the people would shake their heads and say he was mad.

He was the exile of story: a Conrad character.

The Chilian was a trader. He was a little man, with a face, in repose, like a shrivelled crab-apple. When not in repose, it was mobile and expressive to an extravagant degree. One seemed to be looking at one of those faces which the film shows us: the comedian's face in exaggerated pantomime. He was jealous of the Dane, and was anxious to show me that Codlin was my friend, not Short: therefore he brought me gifts, of fish and the rarer vegetables, and otherwise courted me. He had nothing to gain, materially, by doing so; but I, because of my position, was for the time the chief white man of Makemo, and, humanly, he desired my favour. But he was withal good-hearted, and went out of his way to teach my inexperience and to warn me of slippery customers. True, few characters escaped his censure, but if life had made him a cynic it had not soured him. His tongue stripped but his heart was open to all. The natives liked and derided him.

The only other trader was a native, who, in the absence of the priest, was also the head of the church. He must have found his religion a great handicap, for he was an honest, simple creature. But his simplicity was a simplicity of the conscience, not of the mind. For wit he was the match of any rascal on Makemo, and rascality flourished there. William was the one man at the last whom I implicitly trusted.

CHAPTER XVII

*

§ 1

I HAD little enough to do. This was the slack season for copra, and a scarcity of copra made a corresponding scarcity of trade. Of cash there was very little on the island: when the divers returned there would be plenty; but at normal times there is never much cash in the Paumotus. Copra for goods is the basis of commerce there: one weighs the copra, calculates its value at the latest price, and unless the customer demands cash and will not be put off, he is credited with the value of the copra, and allowed to take from the store whatever he fancies, till his credit is exhausted. Thus the trader profits both ways: by sales and purchases, and his sale profits amount to anything up to 50 per cent.

It is not strange that the native submits to this system, for unless he hoarded his money and went to Papeete to spend it, he could only spend it locally at the same disadvantage (as to quid pro quo) as he labours under in taking goods for his copra. Schooners can sell a little more cheaply than shore traders, but schooners call infrequently. Moreover, a good and loyal customer has preferential treatment in the matter of credit. Every customer expects credit, and often the copra brought to the trader is barely enough to pay the debt which has accumulated. As elsewhere, the credit system is one of the causes of high prices, since bad debts have to be balanced by some means; and unsuccessful attempts have been made to abolish it.

The improvidence of the native, his *carpe diem* creed, inevitably brings penury in lean times, and a consequent demand for credit. The result of a cash system would not be to teach the native thrift, which he is incapable of learning, but to make his hardships greater.

My store was just such a shop as may be seen in any back-blocks town of Australia, and not much different from the general emporium of an English village. Drapery was the principal stock we carried; the shelves at the back were loaded with rolls of cotton print for making up into dresses and for wear as *pareos*. There were even muslins and silks. The rest of the stock was of a variety sufficient to provide for all the needs and luxuries of Island life. There were tinned provisions of all sorts – beef, mutton, herrings in tomato sauce, sardines, salmon, jam, fruit, butter, cheese, asparagus; ship's biscuits in immense tins, and the fancy biscuits of Huntley and Palmer in little tins; tea, coffee, sugar, milk, olive oil and innumerable other edibles. There were ribbons, laces, hats, coats, trousers, boxes of fish hooks, hanks of fishing-line, axes, flat-irons, buckets, tin dishes, needles, thread, writing-paper, ink, combs, razors, tobacco, matches, and patent medicines. There were the electric torches afore-mentioned, and there was kerosene. In the warehouse we had coils of rope of different thicknesses, canvas, anchors, kegs of nails, copper wire and iron wire, paint, stacks of flour, sugar, soap, cement and preserved food. In another place, a shed, we had building material. We were clothiers, drapers, grocers, tobacconists, ironmongers, stationers, chemists, oilmen, ship-chandlers and timber-merchants. In fact we were an epitome of civilization in the South Seas. If the health and morals of the natives were deteriorating, and the birth-rate falling, do not blame us: we were but the agents of destiny.

The copra was brought in bags, either by cutter or by hand-cart: there was not a beast of burden on the island. It was then weighed on a steelyard in the copra-house, and as each load was unhooked, and its weight noted, the store-boy who was assisting me emptied the bags upon the copra pile. Before weighing (if the customer were at all a doubtful card) the quality of the copra had to be ascertained: 'dry' copra was what was wanted: 'wet' copra, which is copra imperfectly dried or made from the immature nut, will in the first case lose much weight and in the second case rot. Having weighed the copra, one conducted the customer to the office and made the necessary entries and calculations. He then gave his order, unless the state of his account did not allow of an order, when he had to be painlessly apprised of this and wafted off the premises.

Not only was the island destitute of beasts of burden; it had no four-footed beasts but pigs and dogs. The pigs were of the sharp-nosed 'greyhound' breed common throughout Polynesia; the dogs were large and savage mongrels, usually piebald. I thought at first that they were kept as watch-dogs, and in order to provide sport by their frequent fights; but I discovered that their existence had another purpose. They, as well as the pigs, were material for the oven. The younger and more tender animals were ordinarily sacrificed, but a pet dog was not safe in days of famine. Cook mentions that the Tahitians ate dogs; that is a practice which they have long given up and now deride; but the Paumotuan everywhere is still devoted to it. 'Eater of dogs' is a term of contempt which the Tahitian flings at him – though usually not to his face, for he is also a 'wild man.' To the Tahitian he is what the Highlander is to the Lowlander.

In complexion he is much darker than the Tahitian, and in features inclines to the negroid. Of the two the Paumotuan is the hardier and the more stubborn. His tenacity of life has been tested in many a wreck and cyclone. But it is not so long ago that his diet was fish and cocoanuts. Cocoanuts have gone from it – to the market – but he still eats fish when he wearies of tinned meat or has not the means to buy it. Once, when out in the company's cutter, I noticed that one of my two sailors was very dull and sleepy. I asked the cause, and was told that he was 'tairo' (intoxicated) with eating fish. A fish supper had followed a big overnight catch, and my man had gorged himself. His condition was well described, for it presented all the secondary symptoms of alcoholic excess.

I used the cutter chiefly for visiting the plantation of Maraetefanao, a property which Maxwell's had acquired, about half-way down the lagoon. The excursion made a welcome break in the routine. As the year advanced the weather signs had to be studied beforehand, as violent winds and calms are characteristics of the Paumotuan wet season. Generally we could run down the lagoon on a fair wind (the north-easter being the prevailing wind) and, if it was not too light, be home by sunset. I left the sailing to the sailors. We used to tow a large mother-of-pearl fish-hook, which, by its flashing and spinning, performed the part of a fly in attracting big fish.

Those were fine runs down the lagoon, past the ever changing coast of bay and headland, white beach and lolling palm. The water was studded with *motus* – knobby, varnished reefs of growing coral – and, in the shallows, shot with wondrous hues. Hues unattainable by the painter; jewel-like transparencies: colour spiritualized.

At Maraetefanao I had to inspect the work done since my last visit, land stores and take in any copra that was on hand. To leave copra long was risky, as the honesty of the labourers was not above temptation, and there was no lack of rascals to tempt them. For landing and loading we had a canoe, which was more suitable than a boat for use in the coral shoals, although infinite care was required to maintain its equilibrium. The anxious moment was when we landed the flour; the wetting of the copra would not matter much. From here we sometimes proceeded to Punuruku, a village near the south-western end of the lagoon; and when we went here we had to stay the night. Punuruku was a primitive South Sea village, sans store, sans church, sans corrugated iron. Its palm-leaf huts did not, however, make it picturesque. It was squalid, bare and almost deserted. Life had left it, drawn to gayer centres. Robbed of his innocence, the Paumotuan must now

248

have civilization or perish altogether. The Dane had had a store here once, but his wife's yearning for 'town' life had driven him from it, thereby ending his career as a trader. I saw the melancholy spot which had been his garden; the house he had built; all the pitiful relics of an abandoned home.

§ 2

Capsizes were not infrequent on the lagoon, owing to the suddenness of squalls. We ourselves had some narrow escapes, and many a wet run home in the teeth of a gale. The Paumotuan is an expert and fearless boat-sailer and thinks nothing of travelling from his atoll to Tahiti in a cutter, at the favourable season. Little though he cares for a capsize in the lagoon, the same event at sea is of course no joke. He lives under the shadow of one great danger, the cyclone. Some atolls are no more than four feet above high-water mark. Makemo, which at its highest point is ten, is one of the most elevated. The Dane had given me a graphic account of the last cyclone – of the terrified, wailing women in the church, of families seeking refuge in the tops of cocoanut-trees, of himself and half the village huddled on the higher ground, being pelted with flying débris – and during a particularly heavy blow I thought we were to have a repetition of this. I had gone to bed, having strengthened the cutter's moorings, which was all I could do. The water was then breaking over the quay. About eleven o'clock I was aroused by high-pitched cries and the quick clanging of the alarm-bell, and getting up, saw electric torches and lanterns moving. I ran down the steps of my bungalow, which stood on tall piles, and went 'plunk' into six inches of water. The quay was the point to which every one was hurrying, bending against the high wind. Here the electric torches lighted a wild scene, of straining boats and a wolfish pack of white-caps. A cutter had broken loose and fouled another, and the two, closely locked, were plunging like frightened horses, to the danger of the rest. My charge was comparatively safe at present, and while I looked the immediate danger passed. The fouled boat was torn completely from its moorings and the entangled pair went reeling into the night.

The sea continued to rise until early morning, when the wind, providentially, abated. Daylight showed half the settlement under water; my compound was a lake, and some bags of sugar on the floor of the store were soaked, but that, with the damage to the boats, which were cast ashore and holed, was all the harm done.

On no part of the earth are the sky signs so anxiously read as upon an atoll. In a cyclone a ship at sea is in far less danger; she can manoeuvre, she can run, while the atoll, with no more freeboard, is a helpless prey. Yet men, for choice, live on these isles, as men live on the slopes of Etna. The element of danger has a singularly slight effect on human action; or man might never have exchanged the safety of tree life for the perils of the ground. By his courage, not by his intelligence, which is constantly betraying him into folly, he has become what he is.

Schooners called from time to time, and the coming
of one made a red-letter day for everybody. From the
moment that the cry '*Pahi! pahi!*' was raised, and tossed
from mouth to mouth till the place echoed with it, the
whole village was in a bustle. Girls and matrons put on
their newest frocks; young men swathed their hats in
garlands of sea shells; notables donned white coats; and
children scampered, beating their buttocks in chorus, a
form of emotional expression which their elders no longer
allowed themselves. I myself, as a notable, would put a
coat on, and view the schooner as if she were a bird from
another planet. She completely changed the appearance
of the lagoon; her presence seemed to fill it. If she was
one of our own fleet I had to be busy; copra would have
to be weighed and shipped, and my stock of goods replen-
ished. If she belonged to a rival, I watched with jealousy
and suspicion every movement of my customers. Sometimes a debtor would seize the opportunity now offered of
disposing of the copra which was justly ours and obtaining cash or goods; then I had to use moral restraint—
threaten him, perhaps, with the law. I had entered
heart and soul into my business, you see: had it been
the business of private murder, I think I should have
entered into the spirit of the thing and done it as well as
I could.

Whether the ship was enemy or friend, the obligations
of hospitality were not forgotten. Visits were exchanged,
and we dined and wined one another. I heard about the
war and about the latest scandal in Papeete, matters of

almost equal magnitude. Between rivals trade was barely mentioned.

One of these schooners, belonging to Maxwell's, had a native for her captain, a Dutchman for her supercargo and an American for her engineer. They pulled remarkably well together, each attending to his business. The engineer had formerly been a motor mechanic; had come to the Islands for a holiday and decided to remain here. The ease of Island life was for him its virtue. For the Dutchman its virtue resided in the women. He was a zealous amorist. He pursued women – or, rather, woman, for though they were many, they were all one to him – with the ardour with which a golfer pursues golf. They were his hobby, his recreation, his sheet-anchor: he lived for them and by them. He was wonderfully like a golfer in his simple enthusiasm. Pensive, unassuming and rather fat, there was something engaging about him, especially as he was no all-conquering Don Juan. To be bunkered was a common fate of his. But he played, like all good sportsmen, for the game.

I was troubled for a time with rheumatism, and had a woman, a customer, to massage me. All over Polynesia massage is practised, and its science handed down from mother to daughter. I recovered completely under the treatment.

My masseuse had been the village belle in her day; now she was white-haired and had many grandchildren. Her skin was as brown as a nut, but her features were so like those of an Englishwoman that you would think her face had been stained. Mere – Mary – was her name, and none could have suited her better. Her hair was smooth, neatly parted in the middle and wound in a knob at the back. She had always a smile. Her father had been an English whaler captain, but in mind she was purely native. She mourned the good old days and the degeneracy of her people, the women especially. Paumotu women, said Mere, were becoming as delicate as white women. Nowadays a woman had to lie in bed after she had borne a baby. In former days she would walk into the water, and having bathed, be restored to health and strength.

A peculiar formulary still pertained to confinements. When a woman was brought to bed, it was the duty of her husband to get in with her, and sitting up, take her back between his thighs. In that position he gave her support; the woman, as she laboured, straining against him. In the accidental absence of the husband, an outsider might be called in to perform this office. Jacobi had once been pressed into service. He was new to the South Seas then, a youth fresh from his New Zealand home, and obstetrics being a hitherto unknown subject to him, his modesty had been badly shocked. But he went through his part as instructed, and the accouchement was successful.

§ 3

The Hikueru pearling season ended at the close of the year, and I embarked again in the *Heitiare*. Bad weather started a leak, and part of the voyage was accomplished in a gale, to the clanking of the pumps and the crash of seas. We had a big deck-load of pearl-shell and native passengers, and the question of lightening the ship was mooted; but we struggled into the lagoon of Hao, where the leak was caulked.

Captain Brander offered to put me ashore on another island, where there were prospects of trade, but I was tired of the flat Paumotus and hungered for Tahiti. Its hills, when at last we made Point Venus, were a glad and refreshing sight to me; not for their beauty alone, but because they were hills.

My plans were to have a spell in town, and while there obtain the managership of a cocoanut island, which I knew was about to fall vacant. They partly miscarried, the new manager having already been appointed. Nothing stood in the way of my spell in town, which appeared likely to be a long one. Business was bad; Tahiti was at last feeling the pinch of war. I had a second disappointment when I missed a good billet in the Marquesas Islands, through a more experienced man turning up at the eleventh hour. I was not short of money, but week after week of idleness began to bore me, and hearing that Maxwell's needed a night-watchman, I applied for the position. The management slightly raised its eyebrows, but accepted the offer of my services. My predecessor, I may state, was a sea-captain who had come to grief through drink; my successor an old West Indian negro.

Maxwell's verandah was a favourite rendezvous, and in the early part of the night I had many visitors, people of every degree. After midnight there were only strays, and to while away the remaining hours I wrote. I had not written since I was on the gum-fields. The night as a rule passed quickly; and if nothing now is left of all that scribbling, perhaps those hours were not entirely wasted. When life was awakening on the schooners and the market-going folk began to pass me, I too went to the market and drank my coffee; then to my lodgings and bed.

But this turning of night into day did not long suit me. I slept ill, and my nerves suffered. A rumour that traffic with Australia was shortly to cease decided me to return while the way was open. My arm was not making satisfactory progress, and I considered that I was entitled to a pension for it. Moreover, I had an engagement which my purpose was to fulfil, and it did not seem that Tahiti was going to aid me in this.

I sailed, and have never seen Tahiti again.

GALLIPOLI
PRELUDE

WHAT is this thing you would do?
Would you sing a song?
But why?
Will any man hear you?
Nay, but the gods will hear me,
The old gods of the Beginning,
Of Light and Darkness;
Not man in his grey twilight.
Geb the Earth God,
Nut the Sky God,
Shu the Air,
Ra the Sun,
Rennut the Serpent,
Thoth the Wise,
Hathor and Isis and Osiris;
These shall hear me,
And say, 'Come hither,
Child of the Beginning,
Of Light and Darkness.
Tell us of the earth in these days,
Cleave our weariness,
This flicker of night and day
That threatens grey twilight;
For the merging is the end:
When Light and Darkness
Are no more two but one,
That is the end.'

So I will sing to them
Of the earth in these days,
Sundering light from darkness.
I will sing to them a song of blood.
Of things I have seen and things I have done I will sing to them,
Cleaving their weariness:
And nothing lost if no man hear me.

GALLIPOLI
A SONG OF BLOOD

Tramping feet in the dusk.
Backward the light
Splendidly dying.
Forward the east and darkness.

All turns to shadow.
On the green fields and the water is thrown a shadow;
The trees are shadows;
The carts and the camels and the asses all are shadows,
Gliding by the shadow of a train of men upon the road.
(Dark armed men.)
There is nothing clear but the tramp, tramp, of the feet.
You are in the shadow, tramping feet;
Your day is past, and the shadows have fallen on you.
But did not the light die splendidly?
Aye, so!

Stilled is the city.
Stilled to the tramp of the feet
But filled with shadows.
Tramping feet, say good-bye to the city:
Its delights are turned to shadows.

The sun has gone from it.
Nevermore the merry step for you
In its streets and its taverns.
In fair way and foul way,
In gay way and mad way,
In strange way and bad way,
In rare way and great way
You trod at your will,
But now you are set in a strait way.

Ah, but the sun was bright and hot,
The day was good and the ways were good,
The fair and the foul and the gay and the mad,

GALLIPOLI

The rare and the great and the strange and the bad;
All, for nothing is truly evil –
Under the sun.

Say you farewell to the city of delights,
Tramping feet.
Say you farewell to the desert and the camp,
Tramping feet.
Nevermore the camp for you, nevermore the desert,
Nevermore the City of the Pyramids
(How rosily they glowed before the light died!
How sweetly lay the fields
Closed in the desert's tawny arms at evening!)
Tramping feet.

Clank and rumble and rattle of the train
That carries us away.

Throb and quiver and rustle of the ship
That carries us away and away.
Throb and roll and heave of the ship,
Throb and groan and gurgle of the ship
That carries us away and away and away.

Gracious are your hills, O Lemnos,
But we bide not with you.
Longer than a bird on the wing may tarry we bide not with
        you,
Deep-bosomed daughter of the gods,
For behind us is the day.

Night. Uproar of voices. Tumult in the ship.
Is not our day over, and should we not give tongue
As the birds give tongue at evening?
'Good has been our short spring day!'

Silence. Sleep.
A new day comes, but a strange one.
A red sun shall rise upon us, and the day shall be red,

GALLIPOLI

And we shall see no evening to this day.
So be it. This shall be for others.
We have made them the gift of it.
Gladly we made them the gift, for proud men are we,
Free givers. We were besought and we gave.
Let all men know that we cared not but to give princely,
Yet valuing this that we gave.

Long ships nosing in the dark.
Black shapes of ships
Stealing in the less black darkness.
Black water and the blackness of what is not sky.
Hills, peradventure.
Stillness.
Once again stillness;
As of the inside of a balloon filled with gas
That a spark may ignite.
Not a ripple, not a breath,
But all alive, secretly active, explosive, electric;
As positive to negative,
So the stillness of this to the stillness of death.

Clop!
Quite a little noise as if a pod had burst.
Then, clopple, clopple, clopple, clopple, clopple:
Epidemic and panic among the pods.
Something else, possibly?
Just possibly.
But in the distance. Here pods bursting.
The gas at any rate is crackling.
Its secret activities are germinating.
At last the electric stillness makes itself audible.
And now it detonates,
Shattering itself, reverberating:
A single dominating roar.

Stars among the hills, now hills beyond peradventure,
Against a daybreak sky.
A blue-blackish sky with a light in it

GALLIPOLI

Of a tenderness ineffable.
The hills yet black as blindness starred.
More roars, regular and spaced,
Of a beast taking breath.
Continuous clopple, clopple, clopple,
Rhythmically varied.
The whole a harmony, an undeniable concerto,
To which the long ships steal like serpents,
Curious but stately,
Drawn by the music of the charmer.
Mutely and suavely,
The black ships trail across the sleepy water
That knows no music but the music of the wind
And fears no clamour in its coat of armour.

Light grows, and grows less tender,
Following the law.
The new day is with us,
Come at a glide so subtle that we saw it not.
Day was not and now is,
Full-dressed in his blue and gold.
With a wipe he has burnished the sea's dull armour,
To use it for his looking-glass.
In his young pride he peacocks before us,
And the sight gladdens us.
A day of goodly appearance this our gift.
Bravely it shines, and the shine of it honours us.
Bravely the water glitters,
Bravely the guns roar
And the fountains rise.
Bravely the loaded boats drive at the shore.
The clopple, clopple, clopple, clopple, clopple
Is off to the hills,
But we shall follow it –
If we are permitted.
That fountain spouted nigh. It sprayed us!
Our serpent is disturbed and draws away.
And there goes a boat caught up in a fountain.

GALLIPOLI

How funnily its ends tossed,
Closing like a pair of scissors
And spilling its passengers.
But gaily! Is not this a play?
A water-carnival, a regatta?
With the launches darting, the boats racing,
Spangles on the water, sparkle in the air,
Blue above, blue below, gold and blue everywhere,
Except on the hills which curiously gloom, rejecting the
    day.
Festive it is, but the hills refuse to be festive.
Brooding they are, and sour, and barren and graceless.

Yes, but this is make-believe.
The hills gloom as hills gloom from a back-scene.
Artistic contrast!
This is a theatre, and we are the spectators.
In the water-filled arena is mimic war.
See these ones with infant voices commanding the launches,
From whose mouths issue orders to men.
Look at their gigantic tobacco-pipes!
Were ever infants seen with pipes
But as figures of comedy?
Midshipmen! Tut, tut! Little drolls they are.
Comic relief to the seemingly dangerous spouting fountains.
They are quite unconcerned, these babies.
So may we be.
Let us enjoy the show.
There goes another boat.
This shuts up like a jack-knife, the blade upon the handle,
And disrupts, leaving a dark molecular bobbing residue.
The actors are getting a bath.
But most of them have dived, for verisimilitude –
Eh? They could not get rid of their packs?
So they drown. They would, of course, in ugly reality.
But there is no ugliness about this
We are spectators of an exhilarating show
Perfectly staged under brilliant conditions.
Surely that was a dream of a day for others.

GALLIPOLI

What gift do we make of this day?

What? Is there a rôle for us?
Do we enter the boats and go where the fountains spout?
Unbuckle your belts and loosen your packs, my fellows.
Accidents happen, even at play.

Shall we, or shall we not?
We are halfway.
More. A little more.
Nay, nay.
We are men of dry land. To drown is no sort of death.
We did not come here to drown. It was not in our bargain.
Damned stupid anticlimax!
Ah, shallow water, Lord be praised!
We are spared that bathos.
The mountain conceived of God, but had a miscarriage!
Queer it should stick in the gizzard –
But it was as if the gift should be snatched from the hand.

Who are these upon the beach
Laid in an orderly row in the sunshine,
Head to the hills, feet to the sea?
Their eyes are wide, but they blink not.
The sun roasts them, but they sweat not.
He scorches them, but they do not redden.
Their colour is clay.

Now we know that this is no play.

Look at them. Look not askance.
It is better to know.
We have looked and are wiser men.
They were, they are not.
They were unsubstantial as a dream.

Along the beach we go.
Then into a gully.
We sit. The hour has not struck for us.

GALLIPOLI

We ease our loads and talk, eat, smoke,
Just as on a hundred days before this
When we played at war in the desert.
There is no difference,
But for the clopple, clopple, clopple from over the hills,
And things in the air whining with evil desire,
Rocketing over our heads,
Or sudden on sight of us squealing with fury
And blasting.
But we sit snug and unhurt.
One, indeed, by ill luck, is hurt.
As he goes we note his look.
It is astonished and highly animated,
As though he had been lit up.
From the hills that crowd to the sky others descend upon us,
Men wearing bandages. Very dark, very dirty men.
They stumble and stagger. They too are lit up, but other-
      wise,
They are men who have *fought*.
They are not like us poor clods sitting waiting.
We regard them with awe and veneration.
On them an aureole shines; they have received the acco-
      lade;
They are our own sublimations.
For all that, we are willing to linger here snugly.
Yet we are not happy. We affect to be.
There is oppression in the air.
There is more than the oppression of a blistering sun in this
      close gully.
Our faces, each to each, are a little strange.
(*All* is strange. All *is* different.)
I have a sad feeling.
Tobacco does not comfort
      me.
I miss the brilliance of the water-pageant.
Gone is the sparkle of the early morning.

Listen.
The clopple, clopple, clopple is returning.

263

GALLIPOLI

It is more of a rat-a-tat-tat,
Claiming our ears.
That has a meaning.

Just so. Here comes one running,
With words screwed up in his face.
Orders. Men rise.
We march.

Back to the beach, from which the sun has hid.
(How sombre now the sea!)
Then into the hills.
Were ever hills so gloomy, desolate, savage?
What is this land so morose? Is it of the earth truly,
Or of the barren, bitter, skeleton moon?
This thin, sick scrub is like the scanty wool
On an old decrepit blackamoor's head.
All is a jumble, as if it had been made before form was,
Or botched in the making and left.
This land was never completed.
It is bitter with unfulfilment, vicious with frustration.
There is no hope in it, nor resignation.
It presses hard, it would enter my spirit and defeat me,
Were my spirit not entrenched.
Havoc of the morning!
Gravestone grey above, and around, hemming us in,
Savage desolation.
Evil whining in the air of the things that seek us,
And finding us, burst with their rage.
These things are maniacs,
But cunning, taking us in the open places.
Clatter! Something falls like a lot of old ironmongery.
And that's about all he is, poor lump.
This hill is villainous steep and stony,
And urge is upon us.
Come along, hurry up there! Double up, scramble up!
My ribs will crack if my lungs and my heart swell more.

I am carrying fully a ton.

GALLIPOLI

And these flats, where the maniacs wait for us.
Flats! They are prairies, for width.
And is this war?

Nothing to stab at, nothing to shoot at,
In a senseless jumble of hills that are vacancy incorporate,
Except for those intangible devils of the air.
They have taken a leader.
He goes down ungainly on all fours,
Turning an anxious face as that of a dumb brute,
Dreadly uncertain, piteously beseeching.
(Ah, the horrid shredding of the mask!)
Then – sudden erasure. Gone.
We scramble past it, scuttling.
We have caught dissolution in the act.

At last a living thing beside ourselves.
A minute figure in the tumbled immensity,
High up among the rocks.
He moves by tiny leaps, waving his arms.
He is like a Lilliputian dancing in the palm of Gulliver.
He stops. He is signalling, swiftly.
To us. There is need of us, up there,
To prop toppling battle, keep the brows of these hills
From spilling disaster.
Strain, strain then the more! We want no whip.
We are blood horses.
Miracle, our lungs are freer, our hearts have won room for
    themselves;
And here is a level stretch, and covered,
Before the last heave-up against gravity.
Why, this is pleasure
While it lasts.
Now Atlas, bend again your back.
(What faces! The familiar parodied.
Veils of distortion. Is my face like that?)
But this is the wickedest, yea, by the gods that have no
    mercy!

GALLIPOLI

This hill would curl over and destroy itself, like the
    scorpion,
Of poisonous, crooked-brained spite.
We have no eyes but for the false footholds,
For the loose stones and the slippery clay.
We can no more stop than a clock while the springs hold;
We are machines wound up to go till we break. Automata.
We have forgotten if hills have tops, and it does not matter.
There is a lightness under my eyelids now. What is that?
The sky-line. The sky-line has come down. Or we have
    come up to it.
This must be – the Top!

Halt! Down!

There is nothing here. Still nothing.
Just empty, rolling, scrubby, crumpled inanity.
A country broken with neglect.
A despised land that was never worth notice,
Too long left to moulder in dejection
Now to perk up at becoming a battle-ground.
And where is the toppling battle?
A rat-tat-tat and a crackle on the left is all the sign of it.
Malignant insects waspishly skirl over us,
But the big, whining, blasting devils no longer harry.
This is peace to what was on the way.
This is positive heaven.
We rest. Nothing matters.
It is all past understanding.

We rest. Things begin to matter again.
This peace is astounding, more than anything.
It is untrustworthy; we would rather it were not.
It is the peace of the bravo who lies low to spring.
Behind those bushes are eyes; there are eyes on the ridges.
Once more we have uneasiness, as in the gully.
Action. Let us have action, though it be ill.

We lie in loose strings along the hill-top.

266

GALLIPOLI

The strings stir with the breath of a word that passes,
And as it passes we tauten, gather ourselves.
Wait for the signal. Now. Up!
As a wave gets up
We rise, and the crest of the wave is a-glitter.
We are off!

More of the skirling insects also are off.
While the atmosphere rouses
The landscape stays indifferent and torpid.
We are launched. It was a brave sensation,
Losing intensity
When we seem to be launched into space.
We should like to see an object.
This country looks as if it might swallow us
In pure apathy and absent-mindedness.
It breaks us up, or, rather, we break up in it
Under its awkward, stuck, sodden impassivity.
If it has any design, it is to disintegrate.
It has no semblance of a pattern, but is all rumples, creases
        and excrescences.
An idiot land, as its mate was a vicious-crazy.
It imparts its idiocy, infecting the mind with it;
Giving a tinge of idiocy to the day.
This day has not merely passed understanding,
It reels into insanity.
What are we doing – barging into the country,
Which just gives way before us, stickily?
We are lost in this treacle-tub of a country.
Where are the rest?
But the hornets have not lost us.
The air sings to the tune of whang-whang,
With no individual voices audible.
The hornets have taken many before us to-day.
They lie carelessly scattered, ours and the others,
Those others whom alive we have not yet seen.
Most have a totally restful appearance
As if irresistible sleep had overcome them suddenly.
They are black.

GALLIPOLI

And they have a dusty look.

But here is one who does not rest.
He kneels upon one knee. What stays him?
Did a last will to live uphold him in death?
He is a dim symbol, the single gleam of intelligence
In this chaos of insanity.
He is dead, but he has not fallen.
Death has conquered him, but he has not bowed to death.

High above the whanging twanging hornet song
Suddenly a new note.
Thin, wild, quavering, altissimo.
A cheer!
It pierces.
Our men have struck!
Their cheer is the piercing cheer of piercing bayonets.
We know it, although it is like nothing that ever we heard.
It pricks us; we tingle.
It sheds light upon our darkness, too. It is a beacon in our
    night.
We are not lost; this land has not swallowed us.
There is sanity.
Bear this way. Follow the cheer.
There they are! No.
These are not ours.
They see us and drop behind their bank.
They are few, alone, cut off.
Lost like ourselves, perhaps, in this imbecile country.
No, they are not ours, but they shall be ours!
What came ye out for to see – and to slay?
Behold!
See them, the foreseen, but unexpected.
How curiously unexpected.
All the day have we looked for them,
Yet start when they appear.

It is the moment. It is reality.
Nothing is real till the moment gives birth to it.

GALLIPOLI

And yet this is familiar. We have enacted it before.
There is nothing untaught in our instant procedure.
We do not pause. We stoop low and rush.
They are the goal. We are the ball.
Propelled, we go. There is no more to it,
Except sensation,
Now too dazzling-swift to impress.
That wild altissimo again.
It is ourselves. It is our spirit in the air.
We soar. Death is out of sight.
We are the destroyers, not the destructible;
Born to destroy, born for this moment of death-giving,
Reborn for this reborn moment,
As well known to us as our faces.
Thus in the past a thousand times we fell upon our enemies
With claw, with club, with spear.
Their eyes flinch, they would flee.
It is too late for them.
They would drop their guns and fling up their arms.
It is too late for them.
The madness of undrawn blood is upon us.

We kill.

What have we done? We have killed those who would
    surrender.
Then why were they too late? Can the cat stay her spring
    in mid-air?
The fault was not ours.

They would have cheated us. And our dead are many.

It was an orgie. I will not remember it.
(But I am gladder than I was.)
Wipe off the mess upon your steel.

We move on, following the direction of the beacon,
Which flares distantly again.

GALLIPOLI

My gladness is fizzling out of me
As from an uncorked bottle.

I grow flat. I am tired and thirsty . . .
I wish this field-day would end.
Surely it is time to march back to camp.
We have had enough of these exercises.
We are ready for the canteen.
I could drink a gallon of beer without stopping.
When will the 'Cease Fire' sound? . . .
Oh hell, but this is war.
Am I going to have delusions now?
Shall I be seeing a mirage of pale ale next?
My God, but I would lie down in it!
Come, pull yourself together.
This – is – War.
Unlimited. Calling for unlimited endurance.
Take a prudent pull at your precious warm water,
And don't glue your mouth to the spout.
This day will never end.
It is at least forty-eight hours long already,
And the sun is still high;
And the land is waterless.

No more the beacon flares,
But we have guidance.
We hear as it were the crackle of it;
Its flames roar.
There is a mighty fire ahead of us.
It spreads, by the sound of it, to right and left of us.
In this deep fold of the land it is a sound only.
The hornets are high in the air.
Now another sound regularly punctures it.
One, two, three, four bangs.
Pause, and da capo.
Indeed a lively combustion ahead;
Even unseen, sufficient to wither illusions.
We shall be there.
This day grows more rational.

GALLIPOLI

I have a nascent suspicion there is purpose in it,
At present hidden in the womb.

Over this mangy hog's back – curse its bristles –
We should have view.
It breaks.
An amphitheatre.
But the ring is empty;
The actors are all in the gallery beyond.
We do not stand to gaze:
There is no standing-room up here
For the pests of the air that swarm fanwise upon it.
We hurtle into the empty arena
(Not quite empty: it is opening as a scrap-heap)
And are borne by momentum across it and switchbacked
     up a bit.

The lost whelp has found its dam.

The lost whelp has found its dam beleaguered,
Bloodily snapping at a pack.

The horns of our enemies encompass us.
As the claws of a crab they close to crack us, cooping us
     within.
(Now does the day grow big!)
But why did you stay, brothers?
It was the word.
We have fought with an army this day.
For that went we out, that our brothers who fought
     through the morning
Might hold to their gain of the morning.
We fell on this army and stood in its way.
Safe is the gain of the morning now, dear bought,
And our turn to pay.

Now is the day delivered of its purpose.
Now is all made clear.
And now the hour of the gift's deliverance

GALLIPOLI

Too is near.
(Do you fear?
Nay. There is nothing that cannot be spent, and fear is
    spent.
I have no more fear.)

Take. It was pledged freely and is given freely –
But they who buy me shall pay dear!
I will have my brokerage of them.
They shall wish they had bought in another market ere the
    deal be closed.
They shall make no profit of this purchase. . . .

Now is the end here.
Sing, for the day is over!
(Does a red veil blind you?
What but the curtain falling on the play?)
Sing, for the day is over!
Red the sunset?
Happy omen, so men say.
Red the steel? The pain red-hot?
You dream, my children. All is over.
Death is slain.
All is over, dream or not,
Of gaining, giving, dying, living.
Sing once again.
Birds at evening, sing your lay:
'Good has been our short spring day!'

High in air it drifts away.
High in drifts and dies, dies away.